Seaside

100

A HISTORY OF THE BRITISH
SEASIDE IN 100 OBJECTS

Seaside
100

KATHRYN FERRY

First published by Unicorn
an imprint of Unicorn Publishing Group LLP,
2020
5 Newburgh Street
London W1F 7RG
www.unicornpublishing.org

10 9 8 7 6 5 4 3 2 1

ISBN 978-1-912690-84-8

Design by Susana Cardona

Printed and bound by Finetone in EU

Contents

Introduction 8

1 Scarborough Spa 12

2 Medical Dissertation 14

3 Modesty Hood 16

4 The Dipper 18

5 Royal Pavilion, Brighton 20

6 Marine Villa 22

7 Lodging House 24

8 Bow Window 26

9 Telescope 28

10 Donkey 30

11 Ryde Pier 32

12 Paddle Steamer 34

13 Excursion Train 36

14 Beach 38

15 Parasol 41

16 Shell Grotto, Margate 43

17 Sand Souvenir 45

18 Rock Pool 47

19 Blackpool North Pier 49

20 Toll House 51

21 Southend Pier 53

22 Grand Hotel 55

23 Keating's Powder 58

24 Ironwork 60

25 Shelter 62

26 Cliff Lift 64

27 Volks Electric Railway 66

28 Bathing Machine 68

29 Sandcastle 70

30 Winter Garden 72

31 Aquarium 74

32 Blackpool Tower 76

33 Ice Cream 78

34 Punch and Judy 80

35 Pierrots 82

36 Carpet Gardens 84

37 Promenade Clock 86

38 Tram 88

39 Stick of Rock 90

40 'A Present from…' 92

41 Bucket and Spade 94

42 Deckchair 96

43 Male Bathing Costume 98

44 Pier Diver 100

45 Pier Pavilion 102

46 Oriental Dome 104

47 End-of-the-Pier Show 107

48 Red Guide 109

49 Jolly Fisherman 111

50 Great Yarmouth Hippodrome . . . 113

51 'Oh I do like to be Beside
the Seaside' 116

52 Promenade 118

53 Bandstand 120

54 Illuminations 123

55 What the Butler Saw 126

56 Comic Postcard 128

57 Amusement Park 130

58 Railway Carriage Bungalow 133

59 Head-through Board 135

60 Boating Lake 137

61 Charabanc 139

62 Landlady 141

63 Fish and Chips 143

64 Railway Poster 145

65 Bathing Belle 147

66 De la Warr Pavilion 150

67 Midland Hotel 152

68 Beach Pyjamas 154

69 Walking Picture 157

70 Amusement Arcade 160

71 Palm Tree 162

72 Sun Tan Lotion 164

73 Devon Blue 166

74 Holiday Camp Chalet 168

75 Butlin's Redcoat 170

76 Ocean Liner Architecture 172

77 Lido 174

78 Art Deco Bathing Costume 176

79 Ice Cream Parlour 178

80 Dance Hall 180

81 Crazy Golf 182

82 Barbed Wire 184

83 Knitted Swimsuit 186

84 Barrow Boys 188

85 Sea Wall 190

86 Beach Hut 192

87 Seafood Stall 195

88 Kiss Me Quick Hat 197

89 Bikini 199

90 Surfboard 201

91 Lifeguards Flag 203

92 Caravan 205

93 John Hinde Postcard 207

94 Windbreak 210

95 Flip-Flop 212

96 Clevedon Pier 214

97 Blue Flag 216

98 Tate St Ives 218

99 Southwold Pier 220

100 Seafront Sculpture 222

For Felix, Arthur and Honor.

*With special thanks to Sue Berry,
Helen Bingham, Anya Chapman, Clare Dales,
Andrew Emery, Paul Godfrey, Lucinda Gosling, Fred Gray,
Ronald Laxon, Phil Lucas, Geoffrey Mead, Sarah Moss,
Tim Wardley, Willerby Caravans, Vicky Wiltshire
and the members of my family who spend
an above-average amount of time
at the seaside.*

Introduction

The seaside is more than a place on the coast. It is a human creation designed for the pleasure of visitors. The things we expect to find there today are derived from the preferences of our forbears. Many of the attractions and treats they favoured have become staples of our own holiday experiences. Some hang on as mere remnants, others survive with almost iconic status.

It is these things that form the content of this book. Though few of them are historical 'objects' in the museum sense, they are nonetheless objects of association, things with which the seaside has come to be inextricably linked and whose individual stories come together to tell the larger story of what the seaside is and was.

Despite being surrounded by it, British people have not always viewed the sea in an appealing light. Historian E. S. Turner summed up the prevailing attitude when he wrote that, until the mid-eighteenth century, the sea 'was looked on as something which kept foreigners out and provided fish.' If that was not a terribly promising start, wealthy Britons were at least accustomed to staying away from home at the numerous spa towns that grew up to exploit the healing potential of mineral springs. Whether they chose Bath, Buxton, Cheltenham or Tunbridge Wells, the ostensible health benefit of taking the waters also involved partaking in a social season. With their theatres, assembly rooms and circulating libraries, spa towns were to provide the model for alternative places of resort on the coast.

The subsequent success of sea bathing and the transformation of minor fishing villages into holiday destinations was keenly influenced by fashion. So much of seaside history is about extending the privileges of wealthy people to the masses that this cannot be overemphasised. The rich did not just set trends in clothing; every choice they made was a mark of their status and something to which people lower down the social scale aspired. In Georgian Britain leisure time was only available to those who could afford not to work which made seaside visitors a very select few. This changed during the Victorian era when industrialisation allowed more people to join the middle classes and share the benefits of prosperity. Steam powered transport also revolutionised access to the coast and thanks to cheap railway excursions workers had the chance to experience their day by the sea too. When the government voted in favour of creating Bank Holidays in 1871 the path towards mass tourism was set, though it would not be until 1938 that the right to paid annual leave was enshrined in law. For most British people the prospect of a holiday meant one thing; the seaside.

With every passing decade the numbers heading for the coast grew and the seaside industry providing for them became increasingly sophisticated. New attractions were the lifeblood of resorts and those that failed to repay investors were rapidly replaced. By listing the objects in this book chronologically, according to when they first appeared, it is possible to see not only how fashions changed but also how some things managed to transcend fashion to become seaside essentials.

The sense of a rough timeline also demonstrates key periods of change, specifically the end of the nineteenth century and the 1930s. In design terms these two eras looked very different, copious clothing and elaborate architecture being superseded by a new focus on streamlined buildings and healthy bodies. They are united by the strong spirit of competition that drove resort investment, seen most clearly in the desire to have the tallest Victorian tower or the biggest interwar lido. Taken overall, however, what the object-based history gives us is a window into the layering of seaside traditions as each generation added its own piece to the jigsaw.

Unfortunately the vicissitudes of fashion that made the seaside popular also led to its becoming unpopular in the later twentieth century. There was a clear heyday in the years after the Second World War but when everyone could get to the beach, that beach no longer held any allure for the rich who craved exclusivity. They had been seeking out foreign resorts for some time and embraced air travel to go even further afield. In the time-honoured way ordinary people followed suit as soon as they were financially able, taking advantage of cheap package deals from the 1960s to book a holiday with guaranteed sunshine. This shift had a dramatic impact on British resorts, which lost their confidence along with their core customers. They still had a market but as this tended to be with lower income families and elderly visitors there was less money in the visitor economy to invest in new attractions. Those that were built tended to turn their back on the seafront; leisure centres boasted indoor facilities that tried to mimic the warmth of the Costas through artificial environments that actively disengaged with the beach and the prom outside.

And then articles began to appear in the press about beach huts selling for highly inflated prices, evidence of the late 1990s 'rediscovery' of the British coast. Though the notion of an annual holiday by the sea was still out of favour, smaller seaside towns were beginning to attract people on short breaks. Government recognition of the deprivation experienced by traditional resorts led to regeneration funding and the 'staycation' was transformed into something positive by long queues at airports, global terrorism threats and fears over climate change.

Smart phones may have replaced postcards as the main media for saying 'Wish you were here' but the accumulated history of our seaside resorts survives enough to ensure they still feel distinctively different. That distinctiveness comes from nearly three centuries of attracting visitors, from testing out the latest trends, discarding what doesn't work and keeping what does. It doesn't matter that you can eat ice cream or fish and chips anywhere in the country; it always tastes better on the beach.

What follows is the best of the seaside condensed into 100 objects.

Scarborough Spa

In a time before modern medicine successful spa towns
could attract visitors from a considerable distance, drawn by the
hope of a cure for their ailments. Nevertheless, Mrs Thomasin
Farrer could not have known the impact she would have when,
one day in the 1620s, she noticed water spilling from
the base of the cliff in Scarborough's South Bay.

The rock behind it was stained reddish-brown and when she tasted a little she found the water was slightly bitter. Mrs Farrer was educated enough to sense it might have medical potential and, after using herself as a guinea pig for the iron-rich chalybeate spring, she encouraged her friends to try it.

In 1660 Dr Wittie of Hull penned a book advocating Scarborough 'Spaw', claiming that the Yorkshire waters were good for 'Apoplexy, Epilepsie, Catalepsie, Vertigo... Hypochondriack Melancholly and Windiness.' The only problem was that they were difficult to access. Early health tourists either had to descend the perilous cliff or wait until low tide to cross the beach. In this scenario the presence of the sea was no more than an incidental nuisance. By the 1730s that had changed. Sea bathing had become a custom among visitors and the Spa had been developed to provide more comfortable facilities for its wealthy patrons.

Thanks to the location of its mineral spring Scarborough can lay claim to being the first recognisably modern seaside resort. Traffic to the Spa transformed the beach from the preserve of fishermen, sailors and smugglers into a new social space where visitors could stroll, bathe and ride. Gaming rooms, ballrooms and circulating libraries sprang up to cater for temporary residents and as opportunities for pleasure increased, the popularity of taking the waters gradually declined. At the Spa itself, new buildings devoted to entertainment grew progressively larger eclipsing the South Well and the North Pump Room which, after more than two centuries of use, had closed by 1931. Today Scarborough Spa plays host to live shows, exhibitions and conferences but its history is recognised in Farrer's Bar, named in honour of the lady who started it all. ▨

The beachside Spa buildings in the 1735 engraving opposite were replaced by a far grander venue that was to become the social centre of Victorian Scarborough.

Medical Dissertation

1. Quercus Marina or Sea Wreck, one side with Pods the other side without?
2. Madrepore. — 3. Coralline. — 4. Coral.

For the Georgian seaside to prosper it needed to offer something more than inland spa towns. Since the concept of holidaying for pleasure did not yet exist the answer was to exploit the sea as a new medical cure.

In 1750 Dr Richard Russell marshalled twenty years of experience into *A Dissertation on the Use of Sea-Water in the Diseases of the Glands, particularly, The Scurvy, Jaundice, King's Evil, Leprosy and the Glandular Consumption.* First published in Latin, the book appeared in English translation in 1752 and was on its sixth edition by 1769. Such was its success that Russell is often credited with inventing sea-bathing, if not the seaside itself.

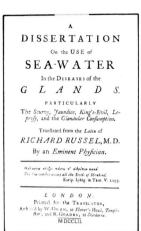

In fact, other physicians had already started to promote the sea as an alternative to spa water. As early as 1667 Dr Wittie claimed that the sea at Scarborough cured gout and 'killed all manner of worms.' The point about Dr Russell was that he was well-connected and lived close enough to London to secure influential patronage. Through his promotion of sea bathing he turned a minority pastime into a fashion. Considering the discomfort of his cure this was no mean feat. Dr Russell advocated bathing in cold water so sent patients from his practice in Lewes to the nearest coastal town of Brighton - in the winter. Once there he advised them to get up early, swallow a preparatory half pint of sea water then bathe before sunrise. After

bathing came a second half pint of sea water and the option of an invigorating rub down with freshly collected seaweed. In order to supervise the treatment of a growing army of aristocratic fans, Russell moved to Brighton where his large new house seemed to confirm the efficacy of his cure.

His arrival could not have come at a better time. Early eighteenth century Brighton was a poor fishing town collapsing into the sea. Bathing gave it new purpose. Other physicians who saw the lucrative influx of visitors followed Russell's example, heading to the coast where they argued for the superior health benefits of their own stretch of shoreline well into the Victorian period. ▪

Modesty Hood

Bathing Machines.

Wheeled changing rooms began to appear on Georgian
beaches as a means of helping health-seekers access the sea
at low tide. In 1735 one of these vehicles appeared
in an engraving of Scarborough's South Bay.

At first contemporaries
were unsure of what
to call them; there are references
to bathing chariots, bathing
wagons and bathing carriages.

Their ultimate designation as
bathing 'machines' came thanks
to Benjamin Beale, a Margate
Quaker who added the mechanical
bit in 1753. His idea was to offer

an enclosed bathing space at the rear of the vehicle. To achieve this he invented a collapsible modesty hood under which people could dip in private. It was an immediate success, quickly copied at other Kent resorts before spreading around the country.

At Margate the system was well run with bathers paying their fee at a harbour-side bathing room where they read the newspapers or drank a dish of tea while waiting their turn. Upon their name being called the bather would descend a flight of steps to a machine which they entered through a door behind the driver. The process of undressing began as the horse pulled the machine into the waves so that, once in deep enough water, the bather was ready to emerge beneath the canvas awning let down by the driver. This four-hooped concertina provided a discreet bathing area of 8 by 13 feet. It must have made for a rather dark and musty space but the desirability of the modesty hood can be explained by the fact that bathing costumes, if they were worn at all, were rudimentary in design. Though the sack-type dresses worn by women were gathered at neck and sleeves there was nothing to stop the skirt bobbing up on the waves. Modesty hoods lasted into the 1860s; the name of bathing machine has endured to this day. ▪

For Bathing in the Sea at Margate,
John & Mercy Sayer *late Pa nem with* M.r Beale
have good accommodations for Bathing,
Where Favours conferd on them will be gratefully acknowledged
M.r Sayer *will attend if Gentlemen &* M.rs Sayer *if Ladies as usual*
N.B By Favour of a Letter Lodgings & Stabling will be Provided.

This four-hooped concertina provided an area 8 by 13 feet, in which bathers could take their sea water cure in private.

The Dipper

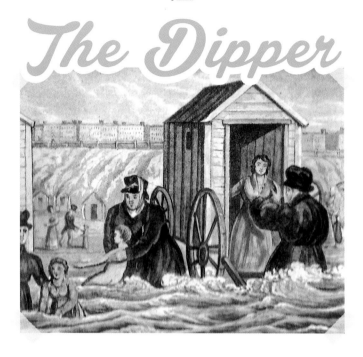

It was the dipper's job to administer the salt water cure.
Though she took her title from predecessors at inland spas,
the seaside dipper became a much more famous,
if not infamous, character.

Few Georgians knew how to swim so the prospect of launching themselves into the sea could be a rather frightening one, not least because the medicinal dip meant exposing the body to sudden cold and a near-drowning experience.

Waiting in the water in her uniform of heavy serge dress and bonnet, the dipper would cajole her client out of the bathing machine into the waves then, taking them by the shoulders, would plunge them into the rushing swell, holding fast against their protests. As the bather's heart raced and the survival instinct kicked in the dipper released her grip. Writing about her first experience of this health re-boot at Teignmouth in August 1773, diarist Fanny Burney declared that 'I had not breath enough to speak for a minute or two, the shock was beyond expression great.' Back in her bathing machine, however, she felt 'a Glow that was delightful – it is the finest feeling in the World...'

The most famous dipper was Martha Gunn, a Brighton celebrity who counted royalty and aristocracy among her loyal patrons. Dubbed 'The Venerable Priestess of the Bath' by a national newspaper, she was doling out sea water on the beach until her death in 1814, aged eighty-eight. Her contemporary John 'Smoaker' Miles was also renowned for his association with the Prince of Wales, earning a royal pension for his faithful service. Though Miles was certainly not alone as a male bathing attendant, dipping was more often viewed as women's work and, in the absence of lifeguards, continued to be an important seaside profession until the end of the nineteenth century. Many Victorian children were introduced to the sea by dippers who brooked no nonsense and left their mark accordingly. The son of American writer Nathanial Hawthorne was handed over to a dipper at Whitby and claimed that ' nothing else is so terrible in the world...to a small, naked, shivering boy as the British bathing-woman.' ▪

Royal Pavilion, Brighton

Royal patronage was the most desirable thing any would-be resort could hope for and the first to confer it were the younger brothers of King George III.

The Duke of Gloucester visited Weymouth in 1765 and the town's reputation was sealed after the King himself came to stay in 1789, the first of many bathing trips aimed at alleviating his symptoms of the madness now diagnosed as porphyria.

Brighton's royal discovery came via George III's most dissolute brother, the Duke of Cumberland, who arrived in 1771 and became leader of the town's hunting and gambling set. When the Prince of Wales visited his uncle in 1783 he took such a liking to Brighton that he installed his clandestine wife, Maria Fitzherbert, then leased a farmhouse overlooking the Steine for himself. In 1787 the Prince's architect Henry Holland turned this building into a much larger 'Marine Pavilion'. With avant garde taste and little regard for expense the Prince continued to build, employing William Porden to create an Indian-style stable for sixty-two horses. Comments that these beasts were now better housed than he was, caused the Prince to begin the transformation of his pavilion into the landmark building we know today.

The Royal Pavilion's design was both fanciful and cutting edge. John Nash borrowed architectural features from recently published books of Indian scenes, superimposing minarets, domes and pinnacles on an innovative cast iron frame. Inside, sumptuous Chinese wallpapers and decorative dragons were combined with the latest technology for lighting, heating and sanitation, as well as thoroughly up-to-date kitchen arrangements. It must have been a truly astonishing sight on completion in 1823

The arrival of court society had a profound impact on the development of Regency Brighton but the Royal Pavilion also had wider influence. The Prince Regent's reputation for rakish behaviour rubbed off on the seaside more generally, hastening

Inside, sumptuous Chinese wallpapers and decorative dragons were combined with the latest technology for lighting, heating and sanitation.

the move away from health towards pleasure seeking. Queen Victoria's tastes were more sober. In 1850 she sold her uncle's holiday home to the people of Brighton and created her own seaside retreat at Osborne on the Isle of Wight. ■

Marine Villa

Pioneering seaside visitors came from the leisured classes, at home in polite city squares and country mansions. These people had time and money to stay for prolonged periods on the coast but the accommodation they found was decidedly basic.

Coaching inns were notoriously uncomfortable so they put up in fishermen's cottages, which at least had the benefit of being picturesque at a time when this aesthetic ideal was coming to the fore. Eighteenth century artist and author William Gilpin described the picturesque as 'that peculiar kind of beauty which is agreeable in a picture.'

When the quaintness wore off regular visitors began building large detached houses known as Marine Villas. The 'villa' term implied a certain grandeur and status but the architectural models were often quite humble as wealthy owners attempted to create new seaside homes that enhanced the picturesque scenery of isolated coastal locations. Popular details included thatched roofs, Gothic pointed windows, gables with fancy bargeboards, verandahs held up by rustic wooden columns and even castellated turrets. Sometimes all of these appeared in a single building. As if to reiterate the point, these villas were frequently drawn for inclusion in books of picturesque views.

The Isle of Wight proved a popular location for marine villas and by 1830 the Undercliff was dotted with genteel residences including Farringford Hill below. Quiet fishing villages like Lyme Regis and Sidmouth, where the villa opposite survives as the Royal Glen Hotel, also found themselves improved by the erection of detached villas for retired people seeking a retreat from society. Such properties continue to define a certain sort of seaside town. ■

The 'villa' term implied a certain grandeur and status but the architectural models were often quite humble.

Farringford Hill. E. Rushworth.

Lodging House

The most common form of Georgian and Victorian seaside accommodation was the lodging house. As coastal towns began to expand local people built their homes with spare capacity to let out in the season and terraces sprang up, like those above at Southend, especially for visitor use.

These were constructed to the standard town house plan, one room wide and two rooms deep, but were generally a storey higher than inland to capitalise on rental income. Affluent visitors took the whole house except for the basement and attic, which belonged to the landlady and her servants. In the second rank of accommodation houses were rented by the floor. Next came the rented room and then, cheapest of all, space in a 'company house' like those in Blackpool where Lancashire mill workers slept three or four to a bed.

Visitors looking for accommodation could find details of lodging houses advertised in newspapers, as well as an increasing array of directories and guidebooks. Enquiries were made by letter but thanks to the spread of the railways it also became possible to send a representative in advance to have a look around and make the booking. Other people simply turned up on their holidays and took what they could find.

Whatever the means of choosing them, the common feature of all lodging houses was that the landlady cooked food provided by her guests. Her rental charge included staples such as bread, flour, potatoes, butter and milk but meat, fish and vegetables had to be bought daily. Luxuries like sugar, tea and wine were placed in the landlady's care though suspicions about diminishing quantities seem to have been rife. The poor standard of meals was also a well-rehearsed seaside gripe but given that a landlady might be required to prepare five or six meals simultaneously for different families who had provided different ingredients, this was hardly surprising. Boarding houses, where all the food was supplied, did exist by the 1770s but took more than a century to become the norm.

Guests provided their own food for the landlady to cook although they usually ate together, as seen here in Thomas Rowlandson's Regency cartoon of a Scarborough lodging house.

Bow Window

The concept of the 'sea view' had to be invented.
Fishermen who spent their working lives on the water
traditionally built their homes facing away from it.

Only after eighteenth century philosophers began to reassess the natural world did Britons begin to enjoy the experience of looking out upon the waves.

In 1759 Edmund Burke set out a new theory of Romantic aesthetics in his book *A Philosophical Enquiry into the Origin of our Ideas of the Sublime and Beautiful.* He argued that natural landscapes with the depth or height to inspire fear should be considered sublime. As 'an object of no small terror' the ocean was placed in this category but the connotations were positive. Through facing their fears head on Burke and his contemporaries believed that they would find personal enlightenment; viewing the changing moods and fearsome potential of the sea was emotionally beneficial. Artists began painting dramatic seascapes as a reflection of this idea and the architecture of new seaside resorts fell under the spell of the bow window.

With its curved profile, the bow window immediately supplied a more expansive sea view, allowing people to contemplate the shore from the comfort of their lodgings. Even properties built along the streets running back from the seafront could claim sight of the

Landlords could charge more for a bow window, giving it economic as well as architectural prominence at resorts like Weymouth, pictured opposite.

sea, something which became an important selling point. John Hudson's 1792 advertisement for lodgings in Blackpool makes this clear: 'Private Parlours to let, together with one fronting the Sea, with a large Bow-window.' Landlords could charge more for a bow window, its economic significance writ large in the terraces of every Georgian resort. It is noteworthy, however, that bowed façades rarely stretched up to the servants quarters, this class of visitor being denied the privilege of a sea view for themselves. At the smartest resorts first floor level canopies, balconies and decorative iron work were often added for extra curb appeal. In the Victorian period the angled version of the deeper bay window took over but the principle of exploiting the sea view remains. ▪

Telescope

SUMMER AMUSEMENT AT MARGATE,   OR A PEEP AT THE MERMAIDS.

As an optical aid for ship-spotting the telescope
had obvious benefits for the seaside visitor.
It was also good for people watching.

Margate's

Georgian bathing rooms provided
telescopes for customers to use
whilst waiting in the queue for
a bathing machine. These were
often trained on members of
the opposite sex already in the
water and satirists were quick
to comment on the presence of

Peeping Toms. In 1813 Thomas
Rowlandson produced his cartoon
'Summer Amusements at Margate
or a Peep at the Mermaids' in
which a row of male spectators
lined the cliff pointing their
telescopes towards naked nymphs
sporting in the waves (above).
Such voyeurism was not confined
to men. In the previous decade

caricaturist James Gillray had also been to Margate where he observed 'young Ladies looking thro' Telescopes at ye Naked Figures in ye Water.'

Many Victorian holidaymakers considered their packing incomplete without a telescope. In John Leighton's 1847 cartoon book *London Out of Town*, Mr Brown refused to take his family to the coast until he had purchased one. Complaints *were* made by bathers fed up of being ogled at the end of a telescope but Edwardian comic postcards continued to treat this as one of the norms of seaside behaviour, demonstrating that Rowlandson's joke still held good a century later. In 1931, however, journalist

Hannen Swaffer reported from Margate that 'the old man with the telescope has lost his job, for in his place are mechanical telescopes! To see through these you put a penny in the slot.' Today the descendants of these early coin operated 'tower' telescopes can still be found around the seaside. Their shape has even inspired a prize winning beach hut at Eastbourne. 'Spy Glass' was unveiled in 2018 as a homage to seaside slot binoculars, the whole hut being mounted on a turntable so users can enjoy an ever-changing view.

This modern seafront telescope can be found along the Marine Drive at Scarborough.

Donkey

Horses were a common sight on Georgian beaches, whether ridden for pleasure or working among the bathing machines. Donkeys were already in evidence too, and donkey races took place at Teignmouth as early as 1773.

Two decades later Margate visitors could put a bet on the donkeys being raced there and in 1805 cartoonists captured the latest novelty at Brighton depicting ladies in Jane Austen-style gowns 'donkey-trotting on the cliffs'.

By 1822 tourists at Margate could hire a donkey for one shilling per hour, this time scale indicating that they were used for more than a mere amble along the sands. Likewise at Weston-super-Mare, donkeys provided a form of public transport before they took to the beach. Early visitors went sightseeing in donkey carts or made leisurely tours of the seafront. By the Edwardian era, however, business had decisively shifted to the sands where a motley crew of flat-capped donkey boys managed more than 100 animals. Almost every resort with a flat sandy shore offered donkey rides for women and children. Since then donkeys have become a much-loved seaside tradition with generations of youngsters taking their turn on the back of Ned, Star, Captain or Champ.

In more recent times there have been significant improvements in the working conditions of seaside donkeys; by the 1980s weight limits had been set, working hours were regulated and days off had become obligatory. Today there are more than 900 seaside donkeys keeping the tradition alive. ■

Whether at Bridlington in the 1880s, pictured left, or at Bognor Regis in the 1970s, above, the joy of a seaside donkey ride is timeless.

Ryde Pier

The UK's first seaside pier opened at Ryde on 26 July 1814. Over the preceding decade of war with France, the Isle of Wight had become a fashionable destination for wealthy tourists unable to get to the Continent. Unfortunately, arriving at its principal port was difficult and undignified. Passengers disembarking at low tide faced a walk of a mile and half over wet sand or the prospect of being carried that distance on the back of a porter.

To attract more visitors Ryde needed a new landing stage. Work began on the timber pier in 1813 and though it was only a simple structure, 12 feet (3.7m) wide, it was the first of its kind to make provision for promenading. Georgian health-seekers were encouraged to take the sea *air* as well as the sea water but their habit of wandering along the beach could bring them into conflict with the fishermen who worked

RYDE PIER.

there. Stone harbours, such as those at Scarborough and Weymouth, proved attractive to walkers and on her visit to Lyme Regis in 1804 Jane Austen followed the trend by strolling along the newly re-built Cobb. These structures existed for commercial reasons but following the example of Ryde, landing piers were increasingly conceived as an extension to the seafront promenade. An 1844 *Handbook of the Isle of Wight* claimed that Ryde pier was now a key attraction in its own right 'from the number and often from the elegance and beauty of the fair promenaders.'

Almost as soon as it was opened Ryde Pier had to be lengthened.

In 1833 another extension took it to 2250 feet (686m), the fourth longest pier in the UK. To improve access a tramway was built alongside the existing structure in 1864. In 1880 a railway pier was added next to that, making Ryde the country's only three-in-one pier. Though the tramway pier was closed in 1969 the rail service still operates, using London Underground trains that began service on the Piccadilly line in 1938. Cars using the ferry service to Portsmouth now drive along the pier and park where a Victorian concert pavilion once stood. ▪

Paddle Steamer

Pleasure Steamer at Pier, Bournemouth

Steam powered transport had a dramatic impact
on the seaside but the change did not begin with the railways.
In 1812 the paddle steamer 'Comet' was launched from its
shipyard on the River Clyde, beginning a new era
of democratic travel.

Three years later Margate
became the first
coastal resort to welcome the
arrival of a paddle steamer from
London and by the end of 1815
a regular passenger service had
been established. Prior to this

the options were either sailing
ship or stage coach. The former
was cheap but so unreliable that,
depending on weather conditions,
the trip to Margate could take
between nine hours and three
days. Though the stage coach

*Setting foot on the steamer meant
holiday time had begun.*

was faster it was expensive
and uncomfortable because of
the poor roads. Steam vessels
won on speed *and* comfort,
with competition between rival
operators keeping fares low.

By the mid-nineteenth century
paddle steamers had become
a well-used form of holiday
transport taking Scottish tourists
up the Firths of Forth and
Clyde, and connecting Liverpool
to resorts at the mouth of the
Mersey, as well as the Isle of
Man and North Wales. Routes
across the Bristol Channel gave
people in South Wales easy
access to the Somerset and
North Devon coast. Setting foot
on the steamer meant holiday
time had begun; drinking was
allowed outside the normal
licensing hours and it was typical

for musicians to get people going
in a sing-song *en route*.

The opportunities for day trips
and steamer excursions expanded
as more piers were built. P & A
Campbell ran its south coast fleet
from the 1890s to 1956, allowing
passengers to hop on and off at
Brighton, Eastbourne, Hastings,
Newhaven and Worthing. Though
the heyday of excursions peaked
in 1914, paddle steamers continued
to be an important form of seaside
transport into the post war years.
By the 1960s, however, they
were being decommissioned in
large numbers. The only seagoing
example left in the world is the PS
Waverley (above). Launched in 1947
and bought for £1 by the Paddle
Steamer Preservation Society in
1975, it continues to make regular
trips around the coast. ■

Excursion Train

THE EXCURSION TRAIN CALOP

THIRD - CLASS
S . E . R .

BY
FRANK MUSCRAVE.

LONDON BOOSEY & SONS 24 & 28, HOLLES STREET.

It is impossible to overstate the importance railways had
in the development of the British seaside. From the 1840s
they carried more people, more quickly to more destinations.

Though proximity to London was a major factor in Brighton's early success the journey by stage coach still took six hours; the arrival of the railway in 1841 reduced it to two. Within twenty years more visitors were arriving in a single day than had previously come in a whole year. Lines were laid to Great Yarmouth in 1844, Scarborough in 1845, Blackpool in 1846 and Torquay in 1848.

As the railway network spun its web from urban centres to the coast, sleepy fishing villages awoke to a new commercial future.

Railway companies were soon offering cheap tickets for special excursion services. The track connecting Preston with Fleetwood opened in 1842 and, that same year, twenty-seven excursion coaches took 2,364 hymn-singing children and their Sunday School teachers on their first trip to the seaside. As the railway network spun its web from urban centres to the coast, sleepy fishing villages awoke to a new commercial future. With its resident population of just 349, Skegness was overwhelmed by the 2,000 'trippers' who took advantage of cheap fares on the first railway excursion from the East Midlands in 1873. After quiet Southend was connected by rail to London's East End in 1889, it surged forward to join Blackpool and Margate as one of the most popular resorts in the country. Some places tried hard to resist this onslaught claiming that rowdy excursionists drove away their more affluent clientele. Most working people only had one day off a week so Bournemouth maintained its treasured exclusivity by banning Sunday trains until 1914. The introduction of Bank Holidays in 1871 concentrated excursion demand into a few peak weekends but outside these times special trains could be hired for company outings. There were so many employees at the Bass Brewery in Burton-upon-Trent that the first trains of the annual excursion began heading for the coast in the middle of the night. In June 1893 fifteen trains conveyed 8,000 workers and their families to Great Yarmouth, where their tickets gave them free access to all the resort's attractions. ◼

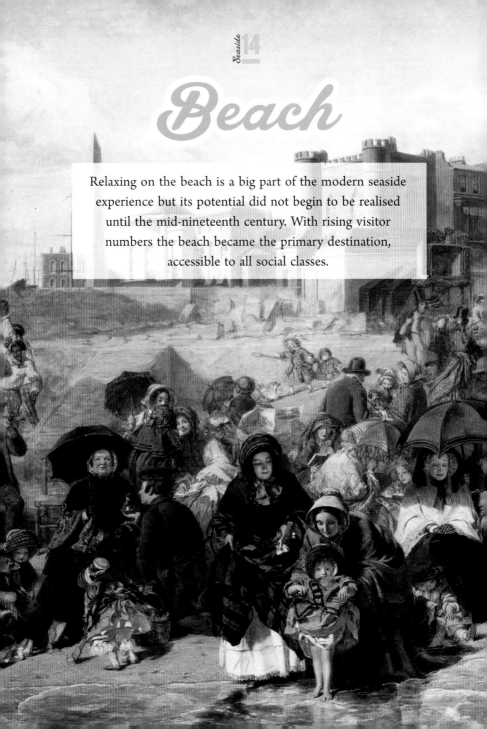

Beach

Relaxing on the beach is a big part of the modern seaside experience but its potential did not begin to be realised until the mid-nineteenth century. With rising visitor numbers the beach became the primary destination, accessible to all social classes.

In his painting 'Ramsgate Sands or Life at the Seaside' artist William Powell Frith captured the bustle of a day on the beach in the early 1850s (previous page). The range of activities he depicts has altered little; adults chat and read as young children paddle and play at the water's edge. The key difference is the extent to which the Victorian beach acted as a market place. Such a mass of people flocking to the sand quickly attracted traders and entrepreneurs so that a visitor to Ramsgate in the 1860s recounted how 'No sooner had we entered, than we heard the din and uproar of several fine ready-money making businesses. "Buy a collar," said the crisp scratching voice of the lady with the blue marked embroidery patterns, ranged out on a toilet-table. "Berries, penny a pint, foine berries!" growled a big fellow, with a truck piled up with red gooseberries that reminded us of sore eyes...' On Great Yarmouth beach in 1877 the loud shouts of refreshment vendors could be heard advertising buns, apples and pears, ice cream, walnuts, lemonade and milk.

Showmen also joined the throng. Among the 316 'standings' recorded on Blackpool foreshore in 1895, there were thirty six photographers and exhibitors of 'photographs, kinetoscopes, picture views, stereoscopes and telescopes,' twenty four ventriloquists and phrenologists, six quack doctors, six musicians and five conjurors. This free-for-all was increasingly subject to regulation and in 1912 Weston-Super-Mare restricted the number of booths on its beach to fifty. Though refreshment kiosks continued to operate on interwar beaches providing tea and a 'tray for the sands', commerce was gradually removed to the promenade leaving holidaymakers to enjoy the beach without interruption. During their 1950s heyday, beaches at the most popular resorts could barely accommodate everyone looking for space. On the hottest days of a British heatwave the same remains true today. ▪

...commerce was gradually removed to the promenade leaving holidaymakers to enjoy the beach without interruption.

Parasol

There seems to be really nobody about.

Most nineteenth century illustrations of the seaside feature ladies shaded by parasols. These were both fashion accessories and an early form of sun screen.

Plain designs in black or white were easy to match with a range of different coloured clothing but brighter choices were available too. For the majority of women unable to purchase a complete holiday wardrobe a new parasol provided a little update to their Sunday Best worn for a trip to the seaside. It could also act as a screen for coquettish flirtations with male holidaymakers or a useful tool for avoiding home acquaintances one didn't wish to meet on the coast.

The parasol's greatest benefit was maintaining a lady's fair complexion. In the nineteenth century pale skin was a mark of status because a tan was something that labourers got from toiling in the fields. Even on the beach fashion dictated that very little of a woman's body went unclothed. The same was true for men. In the 1890s a brief trend for tailored suits allowed women to remove their jackets in hot weather and promenade in skirt and blouse; no such laxity was permitted to their male counterparts who were never seen in public in their shirt sleeves. Flesh was only exposed on the hands and face. Though hats were ubiquitous, parasols provided women with extra protection from the sun.

Ideas gradually changed thanks to the growing popularity of boating, cycling, swimming and tennis, all of which were available at late-Victorian seaside resorts. Catching the sun was accepted as an inevitable consequence of these new pursuits but it was also true that in an urbanized society the poorest people were now the least likely to get a tan. Working in factories and living in slums, their habitual pallor was proof that they could not afford the joys of a seaside holiday. By the 1920s a fashion for Far Eastern parasols made of bamboo and waxed paper was simply that; a fashion disconnected from fears about tanning. ■

In the nineteenth century pale skin was a mark of status because a tan was something that labourers got from toiling in the fields.

Shell Grotto,

Margate

In 1835 a network of passages was discovered
in the chalk beneath a field at Margate.

The story goes that James Newlove was digging a pond for his ducks when a hole appeared in the ground. He lowered his son Joshua in and when the boy emerged it was with marvellous descriptions of tunnels covered in shells. The paying public were admitted three years later and to this day the Shell Grotto remains the most unique and mysterious attraction that the British seaside has to offer.

The grotto's seventy feet of subterranean corridors lead towards a rectangular chamber. The mosaic decoration on its 2,000 square feet of wall surface was achieved using some 4.6 million shells collected from the nearby beach. The native varieties include cockles, whelks, mussels, oysters, limpits and razor shells arranged into a multitude of different patterns. No one knows when or by whom they were collected.

Although tales of the grotto's 'discovery' differ between sources it seems unlikely local people could have missed the substantial earth works required for its creation if the grotto was newly built as a tourist trap in the 1830s. Grottos were popular among the landed elite during the eighteenth century but as status symbols they were always designed to be seen. The Margate example was underneath farmland and unknown even in the immediate vicinity. The fact that the main space features what looks like an altar has led to claims that it was an ancient pagan temple or the secret meeting place of a cult. Marie Corelli, a Victorian novelist who published an account of her visit in 1885, called it 'One of the World's Wonders' and put forward her own theory of its Viking origins. Whoever was responsible, the Shell Grotto survives as a remarkable work of art, crafted from the most humble of materials gathered along the sea shore. ◾

Sand Souvenir

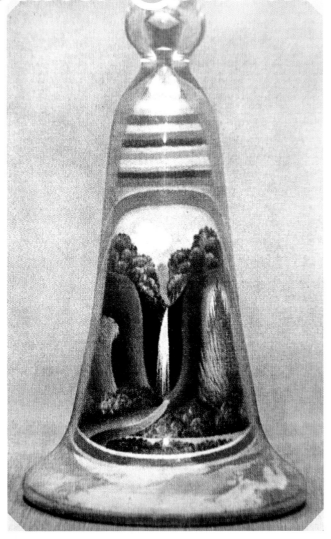

Georgian country houses were full of souvenirs brought back
by aristocratic owners from their Continental grand tours.
When middle class Victorians got the holiday habit they too wanted
souvenirs to remind them of their trip. Some, like Whitby jet,
were highly place-specific.

After Queen Victoria wore a jet brooch in 1850 everyone visiting Whitby wished to take 'something in jet' away with them.

The Isle of Wight equivalent was sand from Alum Bay. Its striped cliffs were described by George Brannon in 1865 as affording an 'extraordinary exhibition of various COLORED sands, clays and ochreous earths disposed in alternate vertical strata – white, black, red, blue and yellow, blending into every variety of tint'. By the 1840s a group of Newport craftsmen were using this sand to create pictures of local scenes to sell to tourists. A more lasting industry grew up around the production of little glass bells which were filled with sand to make paperweights. In 1843 the gardening writer Jane Loudon bought one for her daughter 'with coloured Alum Bay sands arranged

so as to represent the Needle Rocks washed by the tide.' The Queen was presented with two of these ornaments in 1860 which are still on display at the Osborne House Museum.

After a pier was built at Alum Bay in 1869 holidaymakers staying at south coast resorts could take an afternoon excursion to see the famous sands, stopping off at the pier's own bazaar to buy the now famous souvenirs. Damage to the pier in 1927 meant that visitor traffic transferred to motor coaches but the trade in sand grew, with many tourists buying jars to fill themselves. Over a century this human erosion of the cliff had a damaging impact. Modern awareness of this means that the twenty one colours of sand still used to make souvenirs are only harvested from natural cliff falls. ■

Rock Pool

It did not occur to holidaymakers to clamber over rocks in search of sea creatures until the 1850s. That was when a series of best-selling books drew middle class women into a new field of scientific research.

Promoted as a form of rational recreation, the collection and classification of marine animals, shells and seaweed became the newest seaside craze.

Philip Henry Gosse was the greatest populariser, following up his 1853 book 'A Naturalist's Rambles on the Devonshire Coast' with the compelling 1854 title, 'The Aquarium: An Unveiling of the Wonders of the Deep Sea.' His enthusiastic descriptions and beautiful coloured illustrations (previous page and right) entranced readers but it was the breakthrough of understanding how to remove creatures from their natural habitat and still keep them alive that turned him into a cultural sensation. Gosse described how he gathered oxygen-producing aquatic plants for his tank first, returning next day to search for sea creatures to join them. In the ensuing 'Aquarium mania' young ladies rapidly discovered the difficulty of maintaining the right environment; two to three gallons of fresh seawater were required daily to keep fish and sea anemones alive in parlour tanks. Despite the establishment of a London shop to supply returning holidaymakers, the craze proved short lived.

Mrs Gatty's 1862 best-seller 'British Seaweeds' promised the thrill of the rock pool search without the responsibility of keeping live specimens. A year later Charles Kingsley, fellow naturalist and friend of Gosse, published 'The Water Babies' introducing children to the marvels of marine life in a classic story that would ensure they became the chief rock pool explorers of the future. ▓

Blackpool North Pier

Blackpool is unique in having three piers, North, Central and South. The oldest of these is North Pier opened on 21 May 1863 and now the earliest surviving work by the Victorian king of piers Eugenius Birch.

During the 1860s and 70s an average of two pleasure piers were built every year around the British coast. Birch was responsible for more than any other engineer, his final tally of fourteen including Brighton West Pier, Birnbeck Pier at Weston-super-Mare, Eastbourne and Bournemouth.

His first, which opened at Margate in 1855, pioneered the use of iron screw piles to literally screw the upright columns of the pier into the seabed. So successful was this method that after Margate Jetty suffered irreparable storm damage in 1978 the demolition contractors were unable to remove the screw piles and they remain in the sea to this day.

Blackpool North was Birch's second pier and boasted significant improvements on Margate. A continuous seat ran along the outside edge of the entire structure and attractive little kiosks, for use as rest and refreshment rooms, were built on a series of projections that enlivened the otherwise straight promenade. At a time when Blackpool had a mere 4000 residents, the popularity of its new pier was staggering; in opening year there were 275,000 recorded admissions and just two

years later, in 1865, that figure had risen to 465,000. The pier head was extended in the 1870s when Birch added an Indian Pavilion, designed to provide high-class concerts in an exotic setting. Though this burnt down in 1921 the North Pier has maintained its status as Blackpool's most genteel pier. It still has a working theatre as well as a 1930s sun lounge, carousel ride and amusements. It is also famous as the place where entertainer Harry Corbett bought the original Sooty glove puppet for his son.

Toll House

Toll houses were erected with turnstiles and ornamental
gates at the entrance to all fee-paying attractions.
They had two functions; to collect money to repay
investors and to maintain the social tone.

In 1812 the imposition of a 1d toll on visitors wishing to walk along the new harbour pier at Margate sparked a near riot. That the principle was soon accepted shows how quickly visitors came to appreciate the benefit of improved facilities funded by private speculation. When Brighton Chain Pier opened in 1823 its toll houses were located at the start of the

new esplanade demarcating a whole section of the seafront as fit only for those who could pay. In Scarborough visitors to the Spa were prepared to pay extra to cross the new iron footbridge erected by the Cliff Bridge Company in 1827 because it gave them more comfortable access and ensured undesirable people were kept out.

Victorian pier building was entirely funded by private capital so even if no other structures were built along the pier deck there were always toll houses at the entrance. Southport's reputation for exclusivity allowed its pier company to charge an unusually hefty 6d toll and its success in 1860 helped encourage investors elsewhere. The toll to enter Blackpool North Pier was 2d but admission figures were so high that within two years of opening in 1863 shareholders were receiving a 12% dividend. When Blackpool's South Pier opened in 1868 the 1d toll marked it out as a different sort of venture, aimed at a more working class clientele.

Pier tolls remained for much of the twentieth century but were done away with as visitor numbers fell from the 1970s. The majority of Victorian toll houses have also gone but Bangor Garth Pier in Wales (pictured here) retains a handsome pair complete with turnstiles and iron gates that incorporate the city arms. ■

Victorian pier building was entirely funded by private capital so even if no other structures were built along the pier deck there were always toll houses at the entrance.

Southend Pier

View from the Pier Head towards Southend-on-Sea.

The pier at Southend in Essex is not only the longest in Britain, at 1.3 miles it is the longest pleasure pier in the world.

It began in 1830 as a timber landing stage stretching 600 feet across the shallow mud flats of the River Thames. At this length boats had to carefully time their arrival for high tide and it was soon clear a longer pier was needed. By 1846 it had been extended to 7,000 feet meaning that the new steamer services carrying visitors from London could call throughout the day.

Though it has been sliced through four times by different vessels and suffered four serious fires the pier has always managed to defy fate. The disastrous 1881 crash by a barge into the pier prompted a much-needed rebuild and it is the iron structure, begun in 1888 and finally completed to its full extent ten years later, that survives today.

As early as 1833 horse drawn trams were used to carry goods and passengers along the pier. From 1890 an innovative electric railway took over, its open carriages affectionately known as 'toast racks'. Over their sixty years of service these vehicles travelled 3 million miles, carrying some 65 million passengers. They were replaced in 1949 by distinctive green and cream railcars that continued to run into the 1970s.

The pier was integral to Southend's success as a seaside resort. By 1925 over twenty five steamers were calling daily, bringing with them up to 35,000 visitors. Numbers held up after the war but fell away rapidly as a result of mass car ownership until the last Thames paddle steamer was withdrawn in 1963. A decade later the pier's listing at Grade II confirmed its historic importance though little could be done to halt its decline. The public outcry which met proposals for its closure in 1980 began the revival of its fortunes and significant recent investment means that, ships and fires permitting, it looks safe for many years to come. ■

By 1925 over twenty five steamers were calling daily, bringing with them up to 35,000 visitors.

Grand Hotel

Since 1867 Scarborough's South Bay has been dominated
by the monumental presence of Cuthbert Brodrick's Grand
Hotel. A fitting palace for the self-styled 'Empress of Watering
Places' it was the largest hotel in Europe when it opened.

In a boom decade for hotel
building this pile of 6
million bricks represented the
pinnacle of luxury.

Though the Georgians had hotels
they did not begin to differentiate
themselves from coaching inns
until the 1820s. Plymouth's
Royal Hotel of 1819, built as
part of a theatre and assembly

room complex, was the first to
offer seaside visitors a superior
level of comfort. As a new class
of wealthy manufacturers and
commercial entrepreneurs got
rich on the back of the Industrial
Revolution demand grew and
resorts began to provide enclaves
of exclusivity in the shape of
grand hotels. Their very names
evoked splendour: The Queen's

Lowestoft. Empire Hotel.

Hotel, Hastings of 1862; The Palace Hotel, Southport of 1866; The Imperial Hotels at Blackpool and Torquay of 1867. All were prominently situated on the seafront, built on a newly massive scale with lavish interiors, strict dress codes and uniformed doormen. Brighton got its Grand Hotel in 1864, boasting 150 bedrooms over eight floors decorated with 15 miles of wallpaper and served by an army of staff ready to be summoned by 12 miles of bell wire. Three years later Scarborough's Grand trumped it with 300 bedrooms over ten storeys.

By 1900 every resort had at least one of these magnificent hotels. The Gordon Hotels Company operated a successful chain that included the Metropole Hotel at Brighton (1890) designed by Alfred Waterhouse, architect of the Natural History Museum. Dwarfing everything else on the seafront, the red brick and terracotta Metropole had a total of 700 rooms with a wine cellar for 185,000 bottles. Unfortunately bathroom and lavatory provision was less generous. When the pool of cheap female servants dried up after the First World War it was clear the heyday of the grand hotel was over. Conversion to apartments saved some; many were demolished. Of the examples left in hotel use, the Grand at Scarborough remains the most impressive. ■

The V-shaped plan of Scarborough's Grand Hotel was said to be a tribute to Queen Victoria. It is a local landmark and, unlike many of its nineteenth century competitors, remains in hotel use.

Keating's Powder

A-hunting we will go.

In their own homes the Victorians waged daily war on bugs and insects but going to the seaside did not mean escaping the problem. Indeed the likelihood of being bitten was so high bug-related jokes were a stock-in-trade of seaside comics and postcard illustrators.

It was with good reason that fictional landladies often went by the name of Mrs Bugsby. Bed bugs were the worst offenders, so good at hiding in mattresses that they were difficult for even the most vigilant landlady to eradicate. The market for a good insecticide was huge and Keating's Powder cornered it.

Thomas Keating started out in the 1780s with a chemists shop near St Paul's Cathedral, London. In the nineteenth century he gave his name to two new products, a cough lozenge that he sold in winter and an insect powder he sold in summer. By the 1880s advertisements for Keating's Powder featured prominently in guidebooks, advising travellers and seaside visitors to take a supply with them wherever they went According to one promotional leaflet a 'small quantity placed in crevices of the bedstead will destroy bugs, a little sprinkled upon pillow and sheets at bedtime will prevent persons from being bitten.' It came in three

different sizes of tin and was 'quite harmless to animals.'

Sales of Keating's Powder boomed in the First World War when troops took it with them to the front but fell from the 1920s and 30s as modern cleaning products and appliances such as vacuum cleaners began to be more widely available. Thankfully, for seaside visitors, insect bites have since become the exception rather than the rule. ■

Ironwork

Victorian resorts were transformed by cast iron.
As the wonder material of the Industrial Revolution
its popularity peaked at a key moment in seaside history,
when an unprecedented growth in visitor numbers
prompted massive investment in resort amenities.

Piers provided the most obvious demonstration of cast iron's structural and decorative potential but it came to define the seafront in a plethora of other ways.

Along every promenade miles of iron railings were put up to mark the boundary between man-made resort and natural beach. These provided visitors with somewhere to stop, lean and look out to sea and made safe the, sometimes large, gap between artificial sea wall and sand. Railings could also be individualised as at Brighton where they feature dolphins and knights helmets taken from the town's civic heraldry (opposite and right). Fish and other nautical motifs helped reinforce the seaside sense of place and often appeared on lamp standards along the prom. Such iron gas lamps were an innovation that allowed Victorian holidaymakers to continue their promenades into the evening.

Other cast iron structures provided new types of undercover space, specifically promenade shelters and bandstands. Some were bespoke designs while others were ordered directly from the catalogues of iron founders. The same applied to the shopfront canopies of iron and glass that have survived in large number at Llandudno and Southport.

At Brighton the 1890 Madeira Terrace combined sheltered space and railings in a unique structure of cast iron columns and lattice-work arches, running along the base of the cliff for a mile towards Kemp Town. After years of neglect the terrace was threatened with demolition until a successful crowd funding scheme demonstrated how beloved it was by Brighton residents. Plans are now underway to save this important piece of seaside heritage. ▨

Iron gas lamps like this one at Ramsgate allowed Victorian holidaymakers to continue their promenades into the evening.

Shelter

Like beach huts and bandstands, promenade shelters
belong to a breed of small structures that help designate
the seaside as a different sort of place.

Their purpose is to afford
shelter from the
vagaries of our British climate
but they do so with a decorative
flourish that maintains the holiday
backdrop even when the rain is
pouring down in August. Situated
on the paved promenade, they
provide a covered seating area
with sea views, a place to eat
your fish and chips or maybe to

have a clandestine cuddle as the
sun goes down. To maximise their
potential, many shelters are open
on four sides so that tourists can
cheat the wind from whichever
direction it blows. This was
particularly welcome in the past
when it was usual for guests at
boarding houses to be locked out
between meal times. Shelters have
always been free to everyone,

with no barriers or doors and may be, as architectural critic Edwin Heathcote has put it, 'among the most generous and joyous architecture ever built.'

The first promenade shelters belong to the railway age so it is no coincidence that early examples share their architectural styling with the grand new stations of the mid-nineteenth century, combining cast iron with glazed panels and fretted wooden canopies. It was whilst sitting in an uncommonly large shelter of this type at Margate that TS Eliot wrote part of this famous poem 'The Waste Land'.

Designs vary widely across the nation's resorts, incorporating everything from thatch to concrete, displaying changing architectural tastes in miniature. One shelter at Southport is decorated with sinuous Art Nouveau flowers (opposite) while another at Hastings boasts a patchwork of coloured tiles beneath its Modernist concrete canopy. The majority were built from the 1860s to the 1930s but newer interpretations can be found, including 1980s designs at Lowestoft and Skegness. In recent years, the Sussex resorts of Bexhill and Littlehampton have challenged architects to create shelters that maintain the crucial mix of function and playfulness in a twenty-first century idiom.

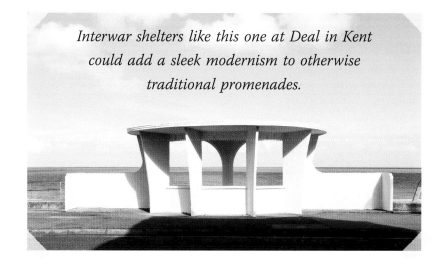

Interwar shelters like this one at Deal in Kent could add a sleek modernism to otherwise traditional promenades.

Cliff Lift

Britain's coastal geography is extremely varied.
Whereas some resorts exist more or less on the same level as
the beach, others are built high above it on the cliff top.

To save visitors walking down to and, more importantly, up from the seashore the Victorians began to install lifts. Whether they are known as cliff railways, incline tramways or funiculars all belong to a rather eccentric and particularly seaside mode of transport.

The term funicular, meaning 'rope or tension', was used to describe a form of cable-hauled rail or tramway worked by a system of hydraulic balance and running on its own private ground. The basic technology was conceived for use in mines and quarries before being applied to passenger transport at the French city of Lyons in 1862. Britain's pioneer funicular opened at Scarborough in 1875 and proved so successful that the resort went on to build four more. Of these, only the original Spa

Cliff Lift and Central Tramway of 1883 remain in operation.

In their Victorian form funicular railways relied on water tanks beneath the passenger cars that were filled at the top station and emptied at the bottom. As the heavier car descended it's greater weight pulled the lighter, lower car upwards by means of a strong connecting steel cable. Water drained at the bottom station was then pumped up to the top to repeat the cycle. The oldest water-balanced lift in Britain is at Saltburn-by-the-Sea, built in 1884 and still carrying passengers over a rise of 120 feet (36.5m) in fifty-five seconds. In north Devon, the funicular connecting Lynton and Lynmouth lays claim to being the longest seaside cliff lift at 862 feet (262m), also still using a water-balance mechanism.

The majority of funiculars now run on electricity including the 1903 Hastings East Hill Cliff Lift which has the steepest funicular gradient in the country at 1 in 1.28.

Other seaside lifts take the form of vertical elevators running in shafts against the cliffside. Though maintaining these can be expensive and several are now disused, entirely new vertical lifts were constructed at Broadstairs in 2000 and Southend in 2004.

EAST HILL LIFT

Volks Electric Railway

Magnus Volk was the Brighton-born son of a German clock maker who loved inventing things. His unique claim to fame rests on the electric railway which he launched on 4 August 1883.

This originally ran a quarter of a mile along the Brighton seafront from the Aquarium to the Chain Pier. Within a year it had been extended and, by running two cars on a wider track, Volk could offer a year-round service every five to six minutes.

Volk's next project was to take his railway the 3 miles to Rottingdean and for this he came up with an entirely new solution. Instead of expensive engineering around the cliffs he decided to run his rails along the seabed, mounting his passenger carriage high above the waves. The peculiar appearance of this salt water tram led to it being nicknamed Daddy Longlegs. Local dignitaries joined Volk for its maiden voyage on 28 November 1896 but less than a week later both of his ventures suffered terrible damage in the storm that destroyed Brighton's Chain Pier. The cost of repairs nearly ruined Volk. Although more than 44,000 people rode the 'Seashore Electric Railway' after it re-opened in July 1897 there were insufficient funds to upgrade the motors meaning it could only crawl along at high tide. In 1902 Daddy Longlegs was decommissioned.

The original Volks Electric Railway proved more robust. In 1901 the line was extended to Black Rock and when the station opened there in 1937 eighty-five year old Magnus was driving one of the cars. After his death ownership passed to his son until, in 1940, Brighton Corporation took over. Today the VER is the oldest operating electric railway in the world, its rolling stock supported by a brand new station, workshop and visitor centre. ■

Today the VER is the oldest operating electric railway in the world, its rolling stock supported by a brand new station, workshop and visitor centre.

Bathing Machine

By the late-Victorian period thousands of bathing
machines dotted the summer shorelines of Britain.

Since their introduction in the eighteenth century they had become the accepted intermediaries between bathers and the sea, a fact which effectively meant anyone wanting to do more than paddle had to pay a fee. This hire charge often included use of a bathing costume as few people had their own. Once returned, the costumes were wrung out on the beach using mangles then hung in long lines to dry in the sea breeze.

...small wheels were fine on expanses of flat sand but where there was a steeper gradient into the water wheels needed to be much larger.

Bathing machine design differed according to the skills of local craftsmen. On the Essex coast they used the same panelled construction as for agricultural threshing machines, whereas at Tynemouth and Whitley Bay their roofs were clinker-built like fishing boats. Beach conditions also affected design; small wheels were fine on expanses of flat sand but where there was a steeper gradient into the water wheels needed to be much larger. This was particularly true along the Sussex coast where wheels could be five feet high.

At Eastbourne, an old machine of this type has been restored after it was rescued from its retirement as a tool shed on a local allotment. Paint scrapings revealed that its walls were originally painted with bold red and yellow stripes (opposite page). This might seem surprisingly colourful but black and white photographs give a false impression of what Victorian and Edwardian beaches actually looked like. At any given resort there could be multiple bathing machine operators, all of whom needed to mark out their machines from the competition. Making them easily identifiable was also important for customers who wanted to be sure of returning to the right changing room after their dip. Though many resorts passed bye-laws to separate the beach into male and female bathing areas the embarrassed gentleman bumbling into a ladies machine was a standing joke among seaside entertainers and postcard artists. ■

Sandcastle

In every sandcastle build there is a moment of tension
as the full bucket is upended, tapped and carefully
pulled away from its contents.

With sand of the right consistency, firm yet damp, the expectation of a perfectly moulded turret is high; where the sand is fine and dry the sides often slip away with the bucket. The benefit of being at the beach is that there is always more sand to try again.

The tradition of sandcastle building goes back to at least 1803 when a Birmingham gentleman visiting Scarborough found himself captivated by the activities of children on the beach: 'To observe the little animals in the greatest degree of health and spirits, fabricating their pies and their castles in the sand, is a treat for a philosopher'. The finished structures could be more or less ornate. Competitive families might vie with other holidaymakers but the real test came when the new cheap national newspapers of the

Edwardian era began to promote contests and award prizes. Alongside such amateur efforts, professional sand modellers were a feature of resorts such as Weston-super-Mare. They sculpted their works of art just below the sea wall so that passing promenaders could throw coppers down on to a waiting canvas sheet. Human and animal subjects were popular as were patriotic themes relating to the Boer War.

For most holidaymakers the joy of sandcastles has always been in the taking part, building with siblings, parents and grandparents, and basking in the glory of shared achievement until the incoming tide does its inevitable demolition work. ◼

The benefit of being at the beach is that there is always more sand to try again.

Winter Garden

Seaside winter gardens were an attempt to cheat Britain's
unpredictable weather. Offering rainy-day diversions
against a backdrop of exotic vegetation they were
a resort must-have during the 1870s.

In their architectural form, winter gardens were inspired by London's spectacular iron and glass Crystal Palace, designed by Joseph Paxton for the Great Exhibition of 1851. Following closure of the exhibition, that building was taken to pieces and re-erected south of the river at Sydenham where it became the venue for huge orchestral concerts. Seaside resorts not only copied the idea, they copied the massive scale too. Southport Winter Gardens, opened in 1874, was described by its architects Maxwell and Tuke, as the 'largest conservatory in England'. Between two enormous brick pavilions its 180 foot long covered promenade rose to a height of 80 feet (24m). The interior full of trees and plants maintained an illusion of permanent summer which also reflected a prevailing middle class trend for educational, slightly worthy forms of entertainment. Bournemouth got its iron and glass winter garden in 1876, the same year that work began on a huge brick-fronted design next to the beach at Tynemouth.

The two great survivors from this period are the winter gardens built for Blackpool and Torquay. Though Blackpool's conservatory element was restricted to a glass-roofed promenade encircling its theatre, the winter garden name stuck as the venue expanded; new attractions including an opera house and ballroom were added from the 1880s. Torquay, on the other hand, was a true winter garden in the Crystal Palace mould but it was built in the wrong place and failed to draw the crowds. In 1903 it was bought by Great Yarmouth Corporation who had it dismantled and shipped around the coast without a single pane of glass breaking. Its pyramid form remains a landmark along the seafront though it is currently closed as the Council seeks funding to return it to its original use. ■

Great Yarmouth Winter Gardens, pictured here, is the sole survivor of the Victorian trend for grand seafront conservatories built of iron and glass.

Aquarium

492   THE GRAPHIC   [*Nov. 22, 1873*]

THE BRIGHTON SEASON—IN THE AQUARIUM

VIEW OF THE INTERIOR

LOOKING AT THE OCTOPUS

THE WATERFALL

THE TABLE TANKS

THE READING ROOM

THE RESTAURANT

In 1853 a Fish House opened at London Zoo with specimens donated by the celebrity naturalist Philip Henry Gosse. It was a ground-breaking exhibit but it had none of the theatricality of later public aquariums.

The first aquarium to give a sense of being underwater was in the Paris Jardin D'Acclimation, where visitors walked through an arcade of top-lit fish tanks in the semi-dark.

The novelty of this experience inspired British engineer Eugenius Birch to design the world's first seaside aquarium at Brighton. Glass manufacturing had industrialised rapidly after the repeal of the glass tax in 1845 and it was now possible to create huge tanks. The largest at Brighton could hold 500,069 litres (110,000 gallons) of water. Accounts of the opening at Easter 1872 described the building's long corridor, its fish tanks set into archways leading to a conservatory and grotto with a water cascade. The biggest headlines, however, were always reserved for the occupants. As aquarium historian Bernd Brunner has put it 'the arrival of an octopus...caused nearly as much fuss as when a foreign king came to town and the death of a porpoise evoked as much grief as a national catastrophe.'

Aquariums soon sprang up at other resorts. Birch designed his second for Scarborough choosing a lavish Moorish-style that delighted visitors when it opened in 1877, while architects Norton and Massey built combined aquarium/ winter gardens at Great Yarmouth and Tynemouth. In 1876 aquariums also opened at Blackpool, New Brighton and Margate. None proved as successful as Brighton. Even by incorporating refreshment rooms and musical entertainment it proved impossible to repay investors and within four years of opening Scarborough and Great Yarmouth aquariums were bankrupt.

At Brighton, the core of Birch's aquarium survives in the modern Sea Life Centre. More recent interpretations of the genre can be found in the National Marine Aquarium at Plymouth and The Deep at Hull. ▪

Blackpool Tower

On Whit Monday 1894, Blackpool Tower opened its doors
to some 70,000 visitors, all eager to be the first to experience
the UK's tallest building and the seaside's newest attraction.

More than 3,000 of them paid the additional 6d charge to ride the hydraulic lift to the crow's nest. In the days before aviation the view from above was truly awe-inspiring and according to the local *Gazette* the most commonly heard phrase about the people below was 'eeh they looked like fleas.'

After the construction of the Eiffel Tower for the Paris *Exposition Universelle* in 1889 a flurry of tower schemes were launched this side of the Channel. Designs were made for Wembley, Brighton, Douglas, Morecambe and Southend. Only the tower complexes at Blackpool and New Brighton were actually completed, both the work of

Manchester architects Maxwell and Tuke. To the top of its flagstaff Blackpool Tower measures 518 feet 9 inches (158m). It took 2,493 tons of steel and 93 tons of cast iron to build the tower but its commercial success was down to the vast red brick and terracotta building constructed around its legs. From its opulent foyers and tiled staircase halls holidaymakers had access to the self-proclaimed 'Wonderland of the World' which included an aquarium, menagerie, roof gardens, ballroom, circus, refreshment rooms and shops. In 1899 Frank Matcham, the most famous and prolific theatre designer of the era, was brought in to upgrade the Tower interiors. His brilliance remains on display in the internationally

renowned Tower
Ballroom and the
Oriental-style
Tower Circus.

Blackpool Tower was
the ultimate Victorian
leisure complex. In the
decade after it opened
other seaside resorts
tried to compete but
none could match its
unqualified popularity.

Despite the massive
capital costs, profits
were so high that
investors were paid
a dividend from the
first year of operation.
Owned by the local
council since 2010,
today the tower is a
Grade I listed building
and an immediately
recognisable symbol
of Blackpool.

Ice Cream

Flavoured ices were recorded in the ancient world
and made their way to Britain via Turkish *sherbat*
and Neopolitan *sorbetti*

Though the first English menu to mention ice cream dates from 1617 it took another two centuries to refine the all-important process of artificial freezing. By the early years of Queen Victoria's reign moulded ice puddings were all the rage at smart dinner parties. However, it was an influx of Italian migrants that turned ice cream into a popular street food, available across London by the 1850s. The subsequent spread of Italian ice cream families throughout Britain coincided with the growth of seaside holidays.

Victorian servings were small, bought as either a halfpenny, penny or twopenny 'lick'. This came in a glass a bit like an egg cup but with a shallow bowl designed to make portions look more generous than they were. Once the ice was licked off customers returned the glass for washing ready to be used again. Scientists proved how unhygienic this was in 1901 and the following year Manchester ice cream man, Antonio Valvona, patented a process for making ship-shaped wafer cups. By the 1920s ice cream cones had become universal.

The twenties also witnessed the introduction of ice cream vans along with the tricycles of London sausage manufacturer T. Walls, who began mass-producing ice cream in 1922 and coined the famous catchphrase 'stop me and buy one.' From the 1960s air-filled 'soft serve' ice cream gained ground under the trade names Mr Whippy and Mr Softy. The history of the iconic '99' is harder to pin down; Cadbury brought out the '99' flake for ice cream sundaes in 1930 and Askey were marketing a '99' cornet around the same time. The Acari family of Portobello claim that they were first to use the name at their ice cream parlour at 99 High Street. In 2007 the familiar image of a larger-than-life, fibreglass '99' was chosen by Royal Mail to illustrate one of its special issue 'Beside the Seaside' stamps. ■

THIS IS THE EASIEST WAY TO KEEP COOL, WE LIKE IT HERE MUCH BETTER THAN SCHOOL!

From the 1960s air-filled 'soft serve' ice cream gained ground under the trade names Mr Whippy and Mr Softy.

Punch
and Judy

Mr Punch is the seaside anti-hero, a clown who entertains children with his slapstick humour at the same time as he amuses their parents with his satirical attacks on marriage, parenthood and the law.

Though he came to the coast on the same trains that brought Victorian holidaymakers his origins go back much further in time to the sixteenth century Italian tradition of *commedia dell'arte*.

Introduced to Britain during the Restoration, Polichenello performed as a marionette for King Charles II and charmed Samuel Pepys so much that the diarist saw him twice in 1662. It was only after his strings were cut that he became the portable Mr Punch, clothed in the uniform of an English jester and perennially armed with a baton or stick. The characteristic Punch sound is also an integral part of the tradition produced by a thin

Pictured left, the red and white striped booth of Professor Poulton announces the presence of Punch and Judy on the sands at Weymouth.

metal reed called a swazzle that is skilfully held in the back of the puppeteer's mouth as he alternates between voices throughout the performance. As the show has evolved so has its supporting cast; the Beadle has been replaced by the Policeman and the Devil by the Crocodile. Judy has been playing the long-suffering wife since the 1820s and still leaves her husband in charge of the baby even though Mr Punch has yet to learn basic childcare skills.

Every Punch and Judy show is the same but different, reflecting the personality of the 'Professor' inside the booth. Even today there are shows that have been passed down from father to son as oral tradition. Richard Codman's Punch and Judy show first appeared on the promenade at Llandudno in 1864 and in the twenty-first century fourth generation Codmans are still saying 'That's the way to do it!' There are easier ways to make a living but seaside Punch and Judy Professors are passionate about their art; the pennies you give in appreciation keep their historic form of entertainment alive. ■

Pierrots

Pierrot Ditti. ..op yer ticklin', Jock."

In their floppy white uniforms, with pompoms
and conical hats, pierrots were a fixture of seafront
entertainment between the 1890s and 1930.

Over 500 troupes worked the nations beaches, performing a mix of song, dance and comic sketches on miniature stages that they built on the sand. On wet days they would often take their shows under the pier.

Early Victorian beach entertainment had been dominated by the fashion for 'Nigger Minstrels', all-male troupes inspired by the US vaudeville act Thomas

Dartmouth Rice, who toured his parodies of Black American song and dance around English theatres in 1836. Unpalatable though it is now, the blacked-up showmen playing fiddle, banjo, bones and tambourine were a music hall hit that quickly transferred to the seaside. In 1890 the French show 'L'Enfant Prodigue' brought a cast of pierrots to London's West End and inspired minstrel banjoist Clifford Essex to set up a new troupe called the Pierrot Banjo Team. After playing to the Prince of Wales at Cowes in 1891, they became Clifford Essex's Royal Pierrots with a summer show at Sandown. Within a season pierrots had ousted minstrels everywhere.

Unlike their forerunners, pierrot troupes included women. They earned their money by collecting from the audience like buskers but also sold merchandise including sheet music and postcards. The most successful pierrot impresario was Will Catlin who went from a single troupe at Scarborough in 1896 to the creation of a seafront pavilion called the Arcadia where his actors appeared in front of 3000 people. He also managed eponymous troupes at Bridlington, Withernsea, Whitley Bay, Cleethorpes and Great Yarmouth.

By the 1920s pierrots had had their day. They were succeeded by concert parties, a change which often involved re-branding the same actors. For example, Jack Sheppard's Pierrots became Jack Sheppard's Brighton Entertainers, their pompom costumes replaced by blazers and yachting caps, with tea dresses and cloche hats for the women. The last peirrot troupe, known as the Pierrotters, was formed in Brighton in 1983 and continues to perform around the seaside today. ▪

They earned their money by collecting from the audience like buskers but also sold merchandise including sheet music and postcards.

Carpet Gardens

The world famous Carpet Gardens at Eastbourne,
pictured above in the 1960s, are a relic of Victorian seaside
landscaping that is proudly refreshed every year.

From the mid-nineteenth century resort councils everywhere began tidying up their seafronts and creating formal gardens to attract visitors. As Fred Gray, author of *Designing the Seaside* has put it, they 'clothed and furnished the stark edge of the resort through a combination of elements', including neatly manicured lawns and paths with ornamental features such as floral clocks. Some places boasted Italian-inspired gardens, rockeries or artificial water features.

Bournemouth was renowned for its Pine Walks but Eastbourne was always the best at using bedding plants to create elaborate geometric patterns reminiscent of Persian carpets. This style of planting was first adopted by

Victorian country house owners who were eager to exploit the new varieties being introduced by plant hunters who travelled the world in search of exotic species. Municipal parks subsequently transferred the colourful displays of carpet gardening to a wider public.

The examples near Eastbourne pier began as the private gardens of a seafront hotel and were taken into Corporation ownership during the mid-1890s. They have changed very little since. Each spring thousands of bright tulips, pansies and wallflowers enliven the promenade giving way, as summer comes, to begonias, petunias and geraniums. ■

Immaculate planting once added bright splashes of colour to our seafronts. It could even be used to spell out messages of welcome as in the display pictured below at Douglas, Isle of Man.

Promenade Clock

Over the years seafront clock towers have provided
the accurate time to millions of excursionists
with trains and steamers to catch.

The earliest and grandest example was built at Herne Bay in 1837 (right) with funds from a rich widow, Ann Thwyates, who was a regular visitor to the burgeoning Kent resort. The core of the tower is brick, its classical exterior clad in Portland stone rising to an estimated height of 77 feet (23m).

The majority of promenade clocks date from the late-nineteenth century when they were a popular way of marking Queen Victoria's jubilees. Those at Margate, Douglas and Weymouth (far right) celebrated the Golden Jubilee of 1887, whilst Skegness, Exmouth and Shanklin erected their clock towers in honour of her Diamond Jubilee

ten years later. As a focal point along the promenade, clock towers are often highly decorative. Brick and stone versions usually favour a Gothic solidity in contrast to cast iron examples, such as those at Weymouth and Douglas, which are more slender and colourful.

Torquay's clock tower was erected as a memorial to the town's Member of Parliament Richard Mallock who died in 1900, while Morecambe's clock was presented to the town by its Mayor, John Robert Birkett, in 1905. These represent the end of Victorian style towers and few have been erected since. A pared down version is Grants Clock, unveiled at Whitley Bay in 1933, featuring a two-sided octagonal clock face mounted on a plain Doric column overlooking the beach. Rhyl's monolithic promenade clock was unveiled in 1948 and stands on the roundabout dividing East and West Parades. At Great Yarmouth a simple four-sided clock was constructed in 1958 to honour prisoners of war held in the Far East during the Second World War. ■

The majority of promenade clocks date from the late-nineteenth century when they were a popular way of marking Queen Victoria's jubilees.

Tram

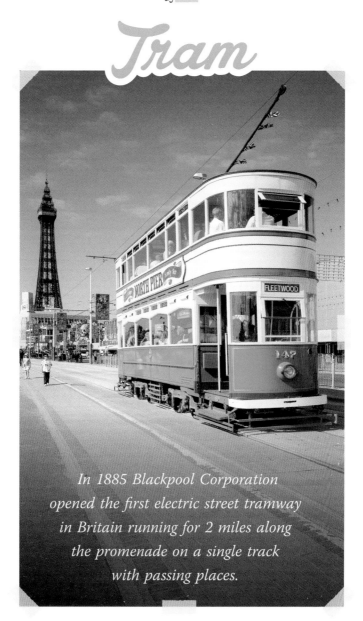

*In 1885 Blackpool Corporation
opened the first electric street tramway
in Britain running for 2 miles along
the promenade on a single track
with passing places.*

When most visitors arrived at the seaside by train their holiday activities were confined to places accessible on foot or by horse.

The introduction of trams allowed them to go further afield. Though horse trams appeared in the UK in 1860, followed by steam trams in the late 1870s, it was electric power that really made them viable as a form of mass public transport. In 1885 Blackpool Corporation opened the first electric street tramway in Britain running for 2 miles along the promenade on a single track with passing places. The original conductor rail that provided power beneath the cars was often out of action due to sea water and sand build-up so from 1899 overhead cables were installed and the tracks doubled to meet demand for the service, which by then had been extended to Fleetwood. Another company ran trams south to St Annes and Lytham from 1903. In central Blackpool holidaymakers could pay 6d to ride the Circular Tour on open-top 'toast rack' trams that always paused on Whitegate Drive for a photographer to take their picture.

Trams became commonplace during the Edwardian period; Brighton got the first of its many routes in 1901, the same year that the Isle of Thanet Electric Tramways began operating a service between Margate and Ramsgate. Great Yarmouth trams began operation in 1902 and those at Scarborough in 1904. By the 1930s, however, their seafront rails were taking up valuable space required by car drivers and motor buses were providing more flexible transportation. Whilst most trams were removed from service Blackpool Corporation chose to make new investment in its trams, turning them into a key visitor attraction and bedecking them in lights during the famous Illuminations. A four year programme of renewal in the twenty first century has guaranteed their future with heritage cars operating alongside the new fleet.

Elsewhere around the coast tram rides can still be had on the Manx Electric Railway operating from Douglas, on the Isle of Man, at the Seaton Tramway in Devon and up the Great Orme to look down upon the Welsh resort of Llandudno. ◼

Stick of Rock

The basic technique of putting words through rock was established by sugar boilers in the early-1800s. No one thought to apply the idea to seaside souvenirs until 1887, when an entrepreneurial confectioner called Ben Bullock took a holiday at Blackpool.

Spotting an opportunity he went home to his sweet factory in Dewsbury, Yorkshire and produced the first sticks of Blackpool rock. He was soon making it for other resorts too. In 1891 *The Daily Telegraph and Courier* described how at Morecambe 'they sell in almost every shop and at the street corners great "chunks" of sweetmeat, pink and white, as thick as a Field Marshall's *baton*, pepperminted to the point of nausea, which they call "Morecambe rock". In Great Yarmouth, Docwra's rock shop opened in 1896; the business is still mesmerising customers with its on-site demonstrations of rock making today.

Every stick starts with a mix of sugar and glucose. Heated to very high temperatures this becomes a workable substance that is divided to make the different colours and layers of the rock. At this stage everything is big, including the hand made letters which are stretched to a length of about 4 feet before being wrapped up inside the 'lump'. This massive sugar sausage, broader at one end than the other, is so heavy it takes two people to transfer it to the 'batch roller'. From this machine

In Great Yarmouth, Docwra's rock shop opened in 1896; the business is still mesmerising customers with its on-site demonstrations of rock making today.

long thin strings of rock are pulled off and rhythmically rolled across a table as they gradually cool into their final shape. Once cut and packaged they go on the shelves.

In August 1945, wartime sugar rationing heightened demand to such an extent that nearly 500 people queued outside Blackpool rock shops waiting to buy their sticks to take home. Rock was even sold on the black market Production peaked in the 1950s and 60s but novelties introduced then, including the rock 'Full English' and the oversized rock dummy, can still be bought alongside sticks in a wealth of colours and flavours. ▨

'A Present from...'

Anyone who bemoans the cheap tat sold in seaside souvenir shops can be reassured that these establishments are following a well-trodden path.

Victorian tourists also loved to spend their money on trinkets, many of which were transfer printed with views of the resort where they were sold. This technique of transferring images from a wet print to a glazed pottery surface revolutionised ceramic decoration from the mid-eighteenth century, allowing unskilled workers to produce cheap items for a mass market. Scottish firms around the town of Mauchline used the same process to embellish items made of pale sycamore wood. In 'fancy goods' shops around the coast the same Mauchline Ware thermometer stands and spectacle cases were available printed with different local views. With the advent of photography, souvenir manufacturers also began using photographic transfers.

In the 1880s William Henry Goss launched a new line of souvenir ware manufactured at his Stoke-on-Trent pottery. His son Adolphus had come up with the idea for white china decorated with heraldic crests and Victorian tourists went mad for it, collecting from a range of miniature vases, jugs and models that ultimately numbered more than 2,500. It is said that by the early twentieth century almost 90% of homes had at least one piece of crested china, though not all of it was genuine Goss.

Imported souvenirs were just as prevalent. German manufacturers accounted for a large share of the Victorian toy market and quickly realised there was a profit to be made at the seaside. Their trademark pieces included porcelain with a mauvish-pink lustre finish and plates with lattice-work borders that could be threaded with ribbons to hang on the wall. Some proclaimed themselves 'A Present from...' while others were made place-specific by tinted transfer prints. Unobtrusively stamped on the bottom, irrespective of whether they purported to come from Rhyl or Weston-super-Mare, were the words 'Made in Germany.' ■

It is said that by the early twentieth century almost 90% of homes had at least one piece of crested china, though not all of it was genuine Goss.

Bucket and Spade

On the beach a humble spade can be turned to a multitude of uses:
digging, burying family members, wheedling-out crabs, drawing
pictures or writing your name in the sand.

For building sandcastles the bucket has yet to be bettered, not least because it can also be usefully employed for shell collection and moat filling. Miniature wooden spades were first produced to get children gardening in the eighteenth century but were turned into essential beach equipment by the Victorians. Matching buckets were less common though they were available by the 1860s; children without these luxuries found the hat of a male relation could stand in just as well. From the late nineteenth century mass production of sand toys began to reduce the price. Tin plate buckets began as thin sheets of metal onto which colourful designs were printed before being pressed into shape. Production increased to meet rising demand in the 1930s and hit new peaks in the immediate post war years when British makers included Chad Valley and ACME Toys. Seafront shops created arresting displays while coastal branches of Woolworths offered buckets in small, medium and large. Choosing from among the decorative range of cartoon characters, animals and nursery rhymes was a holiday treat in itself.

The shift to plastic began in the mid-1960s. Unlike their tin predecessors, plastic buckets do not rust, develop sharp edges or break when they are trodden on. Though they lack the charm of older versions they are safe and durable and continue to give pleasure to children of all ages. ▪

Deckchair

Before deckchairs, seaside visitors were obliged to sit
on the sand or hire a wooden seat, which might be a bench or
a kitchen chair but was unlikely to be terribly comfortable.

It was this, rather than the stereotyped view of Victorians who were 'not amused', that explains the austere poses in early beach photographs.

By contrast, it is impossible to sit up straight in a deckchair. The colourful fabric seat compels a lazy posture that is perfect for holiday relaxation. Its collapsible wooden frame makes it portable and easy to store out of season.

In short, it is the ideal beach furniture. Yet its origins do not lie at the seaside. The deckchair first appeared as an article of camp furniture developed for the British Army in India and subsequently got its name from widespread use on board passenger ships. It was introduced to the sands of Margate in 1898 where it proved to be so much more suitable than all previous seating arrangements it rapidly became ubiquitous.

By the late 1940s Margate Corporation was making 2.1 million deckchair hires every season. It typically cost 3d per morning, afternoon or evening session and customers were issued with a ticket by the attendant in charge. Britain's last remaining deckchair manufacturer, Stephen Davies, began as an attendant himself and recalls how, when he got the job at Portsmouth in the 1980s, the council had a stock of 30,000 deckchairs. When he left in 2007 that number had been reduced to just fifty. To counter this downward trend some councils have tried offering sun loungers as a more Continental option but it is hard to imagine the British seaside without its iconic deckchairs. ▮

Modern deckchairs wait for customers in the early morning sunshine at Weymouth (left) while the striped variety at Eastbourne (right) provide a comfortable seat on the shingle beach.

Male Bathing Costume

Our vision of Victorian gentlemen covered up in neck-to-knee
bathing costumes is only half correct. Though this type
of garment was available by the 1870s men still displayed
a strong preference for bathing naked.

This had been the tradition since sea bathing began in the 1700s but its continuation meant that by he 1860s resort authorities were under pressure to pass bye-laws keeping male and female bathing machines apart. The growing number of people taking to the water excited concern among moralists for the delicate sensibilities of young ladies witnessing things they should not.

A CAKE WALK ON THE SANDS

enjoy a sea bath he must be perfectly free and untrammelled from any costume whatsoever.' The greatest challenge to this view came from well-to-do Britons who had sampled 'mixed' bathing on the Continent and wished to see the practice introduced at home.

Some bathing machine proprietors hired out short bathing drawers and when the first seaside swimming club at Brighton held its inaugural races in 1861, the rules specified that all competitors must wear them. The problem was that, without the benefits of elastic, the drawstring waists were wont to come undone in the water. This practical failing made the one-piece costume seem preferable. Short-sleeved knee-length garments were either buttoned up the front or had wide enough necks that the wearer could simply step in and pull up. Made of thin, knitted fabric they were often striped, the classic choice being red and white.

Advocates of naked bathing continued to defend it until the end of the century, one 1895 writer to the *Daily Graphic* stating that 'For a man to thoroughly

Copying the French and Belgian example resorts favoured by wealthy patrons including Llandudno, Paignton and Cromer began to allow men and women to bathe together provided everyone was suitably dressed. From 1900 bathing costumes were effectively the same style for both sexes, still covering the torso but now with shorter sleeves, shorter legs and a preference for plain coloured fabrics. ▩

Made of thin, knitted fabric they were often striped, the classic choice being red and white.

Pier Diver

PROFESSOR OSBOURNE DIVING FROM THE PIER HEAD, SOUTHPORT.

Male and female pier divers mixed aquatic
and acrobatic skills with a high degree of showmanship,
to attract crowds of holidaymakers from the turn of the century
until the outbreak of the Second World War.

Edwardian high
divers styled themselves as
'professors' and Southport pier
had three: Professor Reddish,

Professor Osbourne and Professor
Powsey. Each had his trademark
stunt. For Professor Albert
Edward Powsey this was the
dive in flames for which he was

covered in sacking and pieces of petrol-soaked cotton wool, then set alight seconds before diving eighty feet into the sea below. Powsey lived to the ripe old age of eighty-nine but his contemporary, Professor Cyril, was not so lucky. On 27 May 1912 Professor Cyril, real name Albert Huggins Heppel, performed his 'sensational bicycle dive' off Brighton West Pier for the last time. Whilst hurtling down the purpose-built slope above the pier deck his wheel slipped, causing him to fall onto the people below and sustain fatal head injuries.

Danger was a necessary part of the act and the next generation continued to push at the boundaries of safety. Stanley Gorton, known as Dreadnought Stanley, had 'his share of hairbreadth escapes' but, as the *Skegness Standard* reported in 1931, 'these merely serve to whet his ambition to go one better than his rivals in the same line of entertainment.' These rivals included the wonderfully named George Daring at Cleethorpes and Bernard Dolphin at Folkestone. Others were born into the profession, notably Daredevil Leslie of Skegness, the son of Professor Gadsby, and world

Danger was a necessary part of the act and the next generation continued to push at the boundaries of safety.

renowned Gladys Powsey, the daughter of Professor Powsey, who was 'said to be able to stay in the water all day'. Other women divers on the scene were Madge Goodall, the star turn at Bognor Regis, and Zoe Brigden, Brighton's amateur swimming champion for almost a decade before she became a professional high diver at the West Pier.

This madcap seaside tradition has its successor in the annual Birdman competitions which, since 1971, have encouraged members of the public to try and fly off the piers at Bognor Regis and Worthing. ■

Pier Pavilion

Grand Pier Pavilion, Weston-Super-Mare

Pier's were originally conceived as walkways
so when a concert hall opened at the end of Hastings Pier
in August 1872 a new precedent was set.

Like the pier itself, the pavilion was designed by Eugenius Birch. It could provide entertainment for an audience of 2,000 and was quickly dubbed the 'Palace on the Sea'. Not to be outdone, the owners of Blackpool North Pier called Mr Birch back to extend the pier he had already built them in order to add an Indian Pavilion. This was completed in 1877 at a cost of £40,000.

Despite their obvious success few other resorts could afford to build a pavilion as part of a brand new pier. That had to wait until the 1890s and early 1900s when resorts that already had a pier got another one. The competitive edge that a concert pavilion gave these new structures led to the rebuilding and upgrading of existing piers. At smaller resorts this might mean adding a simple domed or barrel-vaulted hall but design solutions varied. The 1891 pavilion on Lowestoft's South Pier was in an Arts and Crafts cottage style, while at nearby Great Yarmouth the 1903 Wellington Pier pavilion was uniquely Art Nouveau. In 1902 the Norwich company of Boulton and Paul supplied Great Yarmouth's Britannia pier with a prefabricated timber and iron pavilion, very similar in appearance to the 2,000 seat pavilion that opened on Weston-super-Mare's Grand Pier two years later (facing page).

Unfortunately pier pavilions were highly prone to fire. Hastings burnt down in 1917; Blackpool North in 1921. Particularly unlucky in this respect was Great Yarmouth's Britannia Pier which, over the years, saw three pavilions and two ballrooms go up in smoke. The Grand Pier at Weston-super-Mare lost its first pavilion in 1930 and in 2008 its replacement was also burnt down. It can now claim to have the coast's most modern pier pavilion, opened in October 2010 to the designs of architect Angus Meek. ■

The competitive edge that a concert pavilion gave these new structures led to the rebuilding and upgrading of existing piers.

Victoria Pavilion, Colwyn Bay

Oriental Dome

PIER PAVILION,
HASTINGS

For a long time Western ideas about the Orient were based on an Arabian Nights fantasy of exotic luxury and indolence.

When eighteenth century architects began to borrow design motifs from the East they applied them to playful garden buildings instead of more serious structures. Referencing this tradition, the Prince Regent's choice of onion domes and minarets to adorn his Brighton Pavilion made a clear statement about the building's use for leisure and pleasure. It found few imitators yet when Brighton's new West Pier opened in 1866 visitors sensed a similar Oriental feel in the design of the pier kiosks. There was no model for what pier buildings should look like so engineer Eugenius Birch took inspiration from the most famous local landmark.

Piers proved the perfect place or such extravagant fancy, enhancing the allusion of walking across the sea to another world.

At Hastings (pictured left) Birch took the idea further, designing sensuous onion domes for the toll houses and wrapping his concert pavilion in an ornate iron verandah inspired by the Alhambra in Spain. On Blackpool North pier the domes of the Indian Pavilion were suggested by an open-work structure of decorative cast iron ribs.

Following a lull of two decades, the end-of-century boom in pavilion construction coincided with a Moorish Revival in interior design. Oriental domes became the most fashionable motif in seaside architecture. Resorts in Sussex and Lancashire continued

Morecambe's Central Pier pavilion of 1897 was so laden with domes, towers, arcades and balconies that it became known as the 'Taj Mahal of the North'.

to lead the way. Brighton's 1901 Palace Pier (above) presented a riotous display of domes and horseshoe arches in its Marine

Palace Theatre while, at Bexhill-on-Sea the Kursaal had a Moorish Lounge to match its onion domes. Morecambe's Central Pier pavilion of 1897 was so laden with domes, towers, arcades and balconies that it became known as the 'Taj Mahal of the North'. St Anne's-on-Sea got its Moorish-style pier pavilion in 1904 (below) and yet more Oriental pavilions were projected for Great Yarmouth and Bournemouth, though these were never built. Around the coast, domes on smaller structures such as shelters and pier kiosks confirmed the potency of exotic architecture at the Victorian seaside. ■

Around the coast, domes on smaller structures such as shelters and pier kiosks confirmed the potency of exotic architecture at the Victorian seaside.

End-of-the-Pier Show

The end-of-the-pier show is a shadow of its former self,
now viewed as a graveyard gig instead of the top slot it used to be.

In the 1960s and '70s television comedians could sell out a whole summer season but Victorian programmes were a more mixed fare of music, theatre and variety. Content was tailored to the social class of visitors so in 1890 Skegness Pier presented a show featuring

minstrels, ventriloquist, conjuror, banjo player, contralto and tenor. Targeting a different audience the pavilion on Weston-super-Mare's Grand Pier combined classic drama seasons with visits from national opera companies and Sunday evening concerts by military bands.

Revues came to predominate during the interwar years and by renewing his cast of singers, comedians and chorus girls, Lawrence Wright was able to produce *On With the Show* for thirty seasons at Blackpool's North Pier. In Sussex the long-running revues *Twinkle* and *Fol de Rols* were still drawing large crowds at Eastbourne, Worthing and Bognor Regis well into the post-war era. From the late-1950s Victorian vaudeville began to make a comeback, now called 'Old Tyme Music Hall'. This was also the era when radio and television stars followed the crowds to the coast to perform live shows. Theatrical impresario Bernard Delfont presented acts at piers around the country including Morecambe and Wise, Tommy Cooper and Des O'Connor. Well into the 1980s Britain's best-loved comics expected to spend their summers by the sea. Today comedians are more likely to do a single night as part of a nationwide tour.

At Cromer (below) the variety tradition lives on. Apart from an enforced break during the Second World War the pier's Pavilion Theatre has been entertaining residents and holidaymakers since the 1920s. Its *Seaside Special* has played twice daily every summer since 1978 and thanks to a recent renovation the theatre can now accommodate even bigger audiences for the annual run between June and September. ■

From the late-1950s Victorian vaudeville began to make a comeback, now called 'Old Tyme Music Hall'.

Red Guide

'The use of a reliable guide book doubles the pleasure
and interest of a holiday,' so declared publishers
Ward Lock & Co in 1924.

Ward Lock guides to British resorts first hit the shelves in 1880, with thirty titles bound in green paper boards that came to be known as 'shilling guides' because of their price. In 1892 the covers were changed and the 'red guides' were born. By the end of the nineteenth century Ward Lock red guides covered seventy-two UK and Continental destinations, with every seaside resort of any consequence having its own title. A key sales point was the chain of book stalls first set up at railway stations by WH Smith in 1848 which, by that time, extended to more than 1200 branches.

To keep their guides up to date Ward Lock employed a special staff of qualified editors and correspondents who continually toured the country, compiling

and revising material on all matters likely to interest the holidaymaker. Every town was introduced by a section of local information that listed banks, churches, entertainments, sports and bathing facilities. This was followed by descriptions of the seafront, improvements works, local history, geology and even botany. To complement the highly readable text there were photographs, plans and easy to use fold-out maps. At front and back there were advertising sections including a 'Where to Stay' list. That the publishers had a social conscience is clear from the large number of charitable organisations, whose advertisements asked 1930s readers to donate to seaside trips for underprivileged children organised by the Waifs and Strays Society, the East End Mission and the NSPCC.

In the 1950s the 160-strong range of red guides were given a makeover with new, brightly coloured red and yellow dust jackets. They continued to be the seaside guidebook of choice until falling sales and changes in the market caused them to be discontinued in the mid-1970s. ■

Great Northern Railway needed a poster to advertise their new three shilling excursions direct from Kings Cross to Skegness.

The image produced by artist John Hassall in 1908 has since become the most successful holiday advertisement of all time. Bouncing joyfully across the sand, with his arms outstretched, the rotund figure of a white haired, pipe-smoking old salt quickly became known as The Jolly Fisherman. Hassall got twelve guineas for his work but it was an anonymous railway employee who suggested the famously accurate slogan, 'Skegness is SO bracing', that accompanies it.

Poster art was evolving rapidly in the early twentieth century and Hassall challenged the restrained norms of Victorian and Edwardian design with bold outlines and flat colours. So instantly recognisable did his Jolly Fisherman become as a symbol of Skegness that artists coming after him were simply asked to redraw and update it. In the 1930s Frank Newbould added stylised white clouds above the blue sea and a child pulling the Jolly Fisherman along by his red scarf to promote Skegness as a family friendly resort. That same decade Hassall was invited to make his one and only visit to the town. His original gouache now holds pride of place in Skegness town hall. As an artwork it is said to be worth at least £30,000. To the resort it made famous, the Jolly Fisherman is priceless. ◼

Today a statue of the Jolly Fisherman is a prominent feature of Skegness railway station. He is still the resort's most well-known resident.

Great Yarmouth Hippodrome

Permanent circus buildings experienced a brief heyday
around the turn of the twentieth century. Scarborough,
Blackpool and Brighton all had dedicated Hippodromes
but these were soon converted to theatre use.

The Great Yarmouth Hippodrome of 1903 is unique in still fulfilling its original function. Of the circus rings built in late-Victorian pleasure palaces that at Blackpool Tower is the sole surviving representative. Both rings can be flooded with water for aquatic performances.

Great Yarmouth Hippodrome was built and run by George Gilbert, an internationally renowned circus artist famous for his equestrian skills. Born in Norwich, he made his first public appearance at Great Yarmouth in 1867. Just over thirty years later he was back presenting his own circus in a wooden building on the seafront. This then gave way to a lavish Art Nouveau structure designed by local architect Ralph Scott Cockrill and distinguished by twin terracotta domes over its entrance. Beneath these, three semi-circular windows contain Tiffany glass depictions of chariot racing from the hippodromes of ancient history. The greatest gimmick inside was the sinking ring. In just thirty seconds the 42 foot diameter floor noiselessly disappears into an 8 foot deep well flooding the ring with 60,000 gallons of water. In the early days horses, bears and elephants swam alongside human performers. In 1913 Gilbert presented 'Ardath

and his Alligators' followed by an aquatic pantomime set at Henley-on-Thames which included replica boats that eventually capsized along with most of the cast.

George Gilbert died in 1915 but the Hippodrome continued to operate under his wife's management.

Its next three owners kept up the circus tradition and when

Peter Jay bought the building from Billy Russell's Circus in 1979 he restored the water spectacle along with the original Edwardian machinery that made it happen. Still phenomenally popular with locals and holidaymakers, Great Yarmouth Hippodrome combines amazing seaside heritage with the best in modern entertainment. The synchronised swimmers are worth the ticket price alone. ■

Still phenomenally popular with locals and holidaymakers, Great Yarmouth Hippodrome combines amazing seaside heritage with the best in modern entertainment.

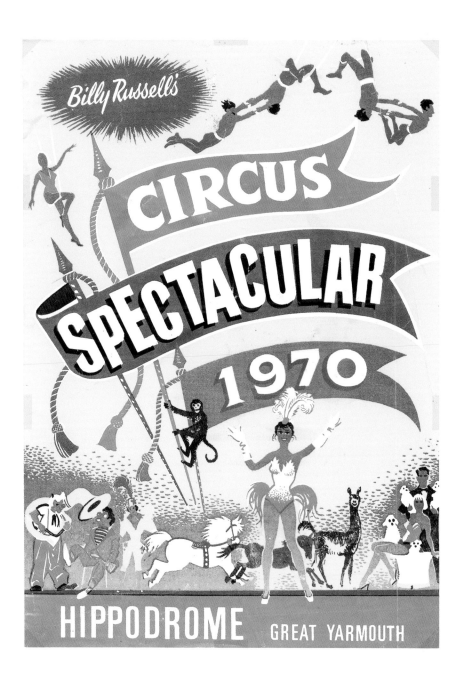

Billy Russell's

CIRCUS

SPECTACULAR

1970

HIPPODROME GREAT YARMOUTH

'Oh I do like to be Beside the Seaside'

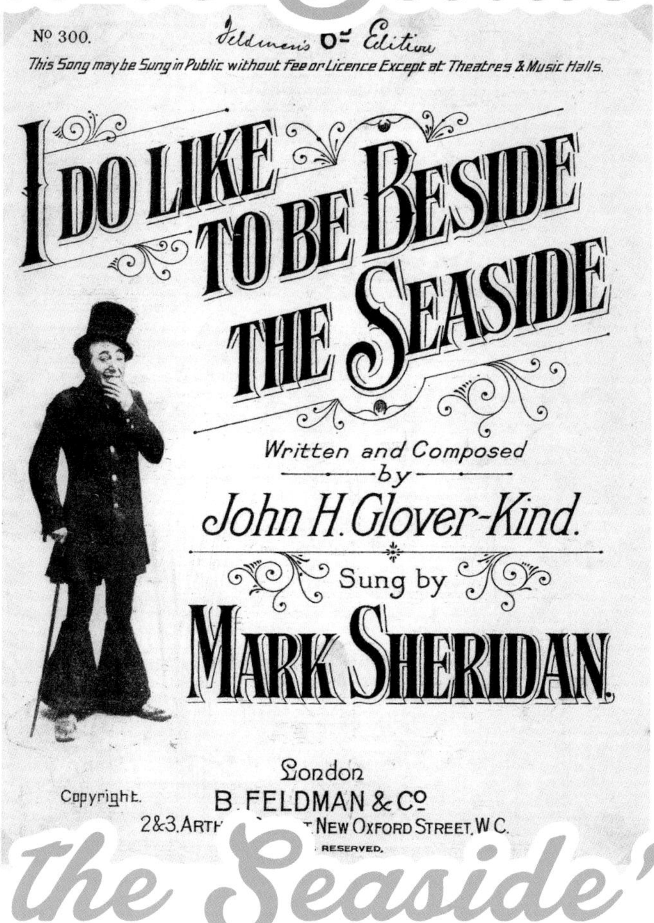

It is almost impossible to read these words
without also hearing the tune in your head.

Written in 1907 by the relatively obscure composer John Glover-Kind, 'Oh I do like to be Beside the Seaside' became a holiday anthem thanks to Mark Sheridan and Reginald Dixon, the two performers who made it their own.

Mark Sheridan was one of British music hall's greatest performers when he recorded the song around 1910. His fame ensured that the catchy tune, with its short simple phrases and foot-tapping rhythm, became immediately popular. It was a perfect communal song for the music hall format but in its lyrics Glover-Kind also managed to encapsulate the allure of the seaside for ordinary working people. His first verse refers to the 'common or garden Smith or Jones or Brown, At bus'ness up in town...

> You save up all the money you can
> till summer comes around
> Then away you go
> To a spot you know
> Where the cockle shells are found.

More enduring are the words of the chorus with its reference to key seaside attractions; 'a stroll along

the Prom, Prom, Prom,' the wafting sound of the brass band and the chance to find holiday romance.

So well-known did the song become that, by the time Reginald Dixon adopted it as his signature tune, the words were unnecessary. Dixon was resident organist at the Blackpool Tower Ballroom between 1930 and 1970. Within weeks of starting there his performances were being broadcast nationwide across the radio helping him to become one of the best-selling recording artists of the period. To this day it remains a magical thing to hear 'Oh I do like to be beside the seaside' played on the Blackpool Tower Wurlitzer. ▪

Reginald Dixon
at the Wurlitzer

Promenade

32602. LLANDUDNO: PROMENADE

The promenade, or 'prom' for short, is a long strip
of paved space that defines the edge of the seafront.

Whereas the beach
may be bumpy with shingle or soft
with sand, the promenade is hard,
the place where you rub off your
feet to put socks and shoes back
on and re-enter the man-made
environment. It is designed for
the use of walkers and is typically
dotted with facilities for them;
food stalls, toilets, shelters and
benches. These days it is shared
year-round with runners, cyclists
and dogs.

From the early twentieth century
resort authorities engineered
new spaces along the seafront,
reclaiming land and building
new promenades on top of
defensive sea walls. For towns like
Bournemouth, developed on a cliff
top, there was a strong impetus
to safeguard the base of the cliff
from erosion but construction of
the Undercliff Drive from 1907
also provided opportunities to offer
new visitor amenities, including the

country's first municipal beach huts. Zig zag paths were created in the cliff face to join upper and lower promenades. At Folkestone the zig zag path was made even rockier by the use of artificial stone Pulhamite but it was always the more refined Upper Leas Promenade that was the focus of the resort's Church Parade. This Sunday institution was also an important social event at Scarborough and Ilfracombe where smartly dressed visitors amassed in a form of social promenading after church.

The human desire to be part of a crowd has long been enacted on seaside promenades where voices and movement become a critical part of the holiday experience. This was so true in the 1930s that there was a fashion for building double-decker promenades offering twice as much space with the benefit of a sheltered walkway for grey days. The example along Blackpool's North Shore features attractive Art Deco detailing while the covered part of the prom connecting Hastings to St Leonards is famous as 'Bottle Alley' because of its concrete wall panels inset with bottle glass collected from local rubbish tips. ■

*It is designed for the use of walkers
and is typically dotted with facilities for them.*

Littlehampton. The Promenade.

Bandstand

The Bandstand, Southend-on-Sea.

Music used to be a vital part of the seaside experience and, until the advent of cheap recordings, it was an experience people expected to share.

From the 1860s to the Second World War British people gathered around bandstands to hear their favourite tunes.

Bandstands formalised music provision in order to get away from the sort of unregulated cacophony that drove Charles Dickens to distraction at Broadstairs in 1847.

He complained to a friend that 'Unless it pours of rain I cannot write half-an-hour without the most excruciating organs, fiddles, bells or glee-singers. There is a violin of the most torturing kind under my window now (time, ten in the morning) and an Italian box of music on the steps – both in full blast.' As the fashion for bandstands spread itinerant musicians formed themselves into military bands featuring brass, woodwind and percussion, distinguished by their smart uniforms and a repertoire that included rousing patriotic marches. Performers and names were often drawn from central Europe, for instance the Red Viennese Band, the Blue Hungarian Band and the Royal Meister Orchestra who all played at Margate from the 1890s. Known collectively as 'German bands' they disappeared overnight in 1914. Regimental bands of serving soldiers also played in seaside bandstands, as did the increasingly popular amateur brass bands established in this period.

Their importance meant that resorts often had several different bandstands, usually made of cast iron. The most ornate were known as 'birdcage' bandstands but even the simplest structures were painted in bright colours.

Musicians were protected from the sea breeze by movable glass screens, a particularly welcome feature on pier bandstands. Their audience sat on deckchairs, with the hire fee going towards payment of the band.

The Leas Cliff Bandstand at Folkestone (above) was built in 1894. Conserved in 2006 it now hosts a lively summer season of band performances.

As tastes changed between the wars Victorian iron bandstands gave way to semi-circular band enclosures built using concrete and faïence. Many of these structures are now also lost but examples remain at Worthing, Herne Bay and Ramsgate. The most enduringly popular opened on 5 August 1935 at Eastbourne and regular concerts continue to be held there. ■

With its turquoise tiled roof, Eastbourne's bandstand remains a popular music venue. Like many other interwar examples it was built at the centre of a band enclosure to keep the audience sheltered from sea breezes

Illuminations

The History of the Lights....

Large scale outdoor illuminations were pioneered by Blackpool in 1912, curtailed by the 1914/18 war and remained dormant until revived in 1925. Displays then continued annually until 1938 when war again interrupted the sequence. Staged again in 1949 they have become one of Blackpool's major attractions.

This Autumn's Illuminations are even more attractive and fascinating than ever before and provide an outstanding lighting and electrical extravaganza.

The British summer season has always been notoriously short with its peak during late July and August. Research in the 1930s found that even if working people had a choice of when to take annual leave the majority would favour the traditional summer months.

For seaside resorts this meant making the bulk of their annual profits in the space of six weeks.

The most successful ruse to extend the season came courtesy of electric lighting which was used to create spectacular autumn displays at many mid-twentieth century resorts. Parks and promenades were lit up from Margate to Morecambe but it was at Blackpool that the Illuminations proved most abiding.

Blackpool promenade was first lit up in May 1912 to celebrate the visit of Her Royal Highness Princess Louise. The experiment was so successful it was repeated the following year during September and early October. After a lengthy gap caused by the First World War the Illuminations were back in 1925 and within two years were attracting national press headlines for 'Taking the Black out of Blackpool' and providing 'A month of Aladdin Nights.' Innovative neon lights and animated tableaux meant that by 1936 the town welcomed 900,000 extra autumn visitors. To design, build and put up the 140 different types of lamp and twenty seven miles of strip lighting the Council employed a seasonal workforce of more than 100 men.

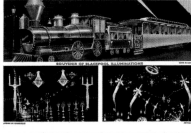

During the 'Golden Age of Lights' in the 1950s and 60s fibre glass and plastic were introduced to add 3D figures to the displays. Blackpool Council did a deal with Disney to promote its films using art work supplied by the American studios and the 'Switch on' became a show in its own right, performed by celebrities in front of BBC television cameras. Despite financial constraints in the 1980s that killed off Illuminations at other resorts, the bright lights of Blackpool continued to shine and by the late 1990s were attracting up to 5 million people. Today the Illuminations Department has its own purpose-built depot where more energy efficient displays are put together from a mixture of new themes and restored favourites from the past. ▪

To design, build and put up the 140 different types of lamp and twenty seven miles of strip lighting the Council employed a seasonal workforce of more than 100 men.

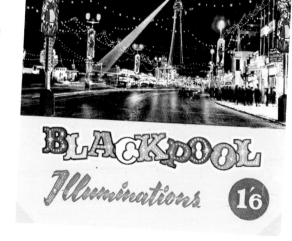

What the Butler Saw

In 1894 American inventor Herman Casler patented
the Mutoscope, an early predecessor of moving pictures
based on the 'flip book' principle.

Within four years
mutoscopes
were being manufactured in
Britain, finding a ready audience
at the seaside, particularly
on piers.

Inside each mutoscope some 850
photographs were sequentially
mounted around a circular
drum, flipping from one to the
next to give the impression of
movement as the viewer turned

a crank handle on the side. For a penny, holidaymakers got a minute's worth of entertainment. Themes were often risqué, with titillating titles and mild striptease that exploited the sensation of peeping in on private moments. One of the most popular early mutoscope titles made reference to the scandalous divorce case of Lord Colin Campbell and Gertrude Elizabeth Blood in 1886, when jurors were taken to the couple's London home to peer through the keyhole used by the butler to witness Gertrude's alleged infidelity. Though there was no evidence to grant the divorce the story lived on in popular culture ultimately inspiring the mutoscope's alternative name of 'What the Butler Saw'.

Other titles with early erotic content included 'Parisian Can-Can', 'The Hula-Dancer' and 'The Naked Truth' though these often promised more than they delivered. Rows of seaside mutoscopes remained popular until the introduction of decimal coinage in 1971 when converting them to new money proved difficult. Though the majority of What the Butler Saw machines were scrapped, survivors still exist in heritage collections. ■

Themes were often risqué, with titillating titles and mild striptease that exploited the sensation of peeping in on private moments.

Comic Postcard

Royal Mail gave British publishers permission to manufacture and distribute picture postcards in 1894.

They were the perfect holiday souvenir and helpfully undemanding as a means of corresponding with the folks at home, requiring just a few short words written on the back. Early examples focussed on scenic views but with the employment of postcard illustrators a new form of comic postcard was born.

Seaside pastimes had been satirised by cartoonists since the Georgian era, the difference now was the massive growth in audience. Puns, innuendo and stereotypes were all used to humorous effect in Edwardian cards depicting landladies, overcrowded lodgings, 'mixed' male and female bathing and holiday romance. By the early 1930s cartoon-style cards had become widespread; at their peak some 16 million were produced every year.

The most famous postcard artist was Donald McGill who created over 12,000 cards in a career that lasted from 1904 to 1962. Not only was he supremely skilled at seeing the joke in every situation, he was able to keep his innuendo on the right side of public decency. It was an acknowledged fact that standards were stretched at the seaside,

Fearful of moral decline the ruling Conservative party led a crackdown on saucy seaside postcards.

ADVICE TO GIRLS AT THE SEASIDE.

THE GIRL WHO TOOK THE WRONG TURNING ON THE PIER EVERY EVENING

WHEN HAVING YOUR PHOTO TAKEN ON THE BEACH BE CAREFUL ABOUT THE BACKGROUND.

on the edge of normal moral codes as well as the country, but in the early 1950s this reputation for laxity came under government scrutiny. Fearful of moral decline the ruling Conservative party led a crackdown on saucy seaside postcards. McGill became a target and in 1954 he was fined for violating obscenity laws. The police were given powers to confiscate postcards so resort authorities stayed one step ahead by establishing their own censorship committees. The subjectivity of what was decent, however, meant that a postcard which was rejected by Blackpool censors might be allowed in Hastings or Brighton!

In the more liberal 1960s it was back to business as usual. Big boobs and *double entendres* were the stock in trade of cards that sold a two dimensional version of Carry On humour. Their demise began in the following decade, as saucy postcards fell out of fashion along with the seaside they affectionately mocked. Their value as a phenomenally successful branch of commercial art is still to be fully recognised but for their commentary on our seaside past they are invaluable. ▪

Amusement Park

Casino and Pleasure Beach, S. S. Blackpool

Before seaside outings ordinary people got their holiday fun courtesy of travelling fairs. As more and more workers quit their home towns each summer, permanent fairgrounds were established by the sea.

Rides became a feature of resorts from the 1880s but in the 1900s they began to be grouped together in amusement parks.

Blackpool Pleasure Beach was one of the earliest and remains the most successful, tracing its origins to a late-Victorian gypsy encampment among the sand dunes. At the end of the tram line it was easy to get to but the land was cheap enough to allow for expansion as big new attractions were introduced from America.

In 1904 that meant Hiram Maxim's 'Captive Flying Machine', a ride which is still speeding visitors through the air today. Three years later it was joined by the Scenic Railway, an early form of wooden roller coaster, which travelled faster than Edwardian cars at a speed of 35 mph. 1906 saw the creation of Morecambe's West End Amusement Park while a sister park to Blackpool Pleasure Beach opened at Southport in 1913.

The real expansion period happened between the wars. Margate's Victorian 'Hall by the Sea' was relaunched as Dreamland, defined by the iconic Art Deco fin of its seafront cinema building. At Southend the Edwardian Kursaal was transformed into a massive new amusement park. Architect Joseph Emberton gave Blackpool Pleasure Beach a stunning streamlined makeover and Billy Butlin launched his seaside empire with an amusement park at Skegness that became the beginning of a coast-wide chain.

Millions of holidaymakers returned to these parks after

Margate's Victorian 'Hall by the Sea' was relaunched as Dreamland, defined by the iconic Art Deco fin of its seafront cinema building.

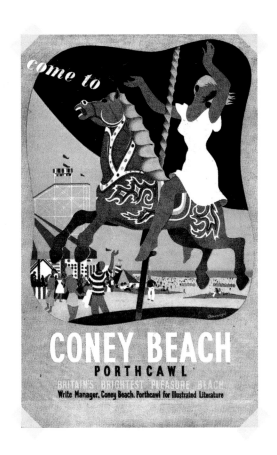

the Second World War but it proved hard to maintain and update them as visitor numbers declined in the late twentieth century. Whereas many parks closed, Blackpool Pleasure Beach continued to innovate, investing in new attractions, most recently with 'Icon', the UK's first double launch roller coaster, which opened in May 2018 at a cost of £16.25 million. At Margate, the much-publicised restoration of Dreamland has seen its 1919 scenic railway become the focus for a vintage theme park while at Great Yarmouth Pleasure Beach the country's second oldest wooden roller coaster, installed in 1932, is still going strong. ■

Railway Carriage

Bungalow

Victorian fishermen were the first to use redundant train carriages on the beach, turning them into net stores along the shingle at Shoreham, near Brighton.

Inspired by their example a local entrepreneur had the idea of letting out the beach for holiday accommodation, subdividing it into 66 square foot plots and making a deal with the London, Brighton & South Coast Railway to supply old carriages for conversion. The first of these arrived and was turned into a bungalow around 1884. By 1900 Shoreham 'Bungalow Town' consisted of 150 properties stretching a mile and a half along the beach.

Bungalows originally came from India; the name derives from the Hindi or Mahratti term *bangla,* meaning 'of or belonging to Bengal'. British colonials adapted the native Bengali hut for their own use and from the 1850s this type of Anglo-Indian bungalow began to appear in Britain. Pioneering seaside bungalows at Westgate-on-Sea and Birchington in Kent set the tone for early developments, bought by wealthy Londoners looking for a Bohemian alternative to crowded resorts.

As holiday bungalows became fashionable the use of old rolling stock offered a cheaper option. In 1900 a passenger carriage could be had for £10-12. Two of these would provide the outside walls of a bungalow with space in between roofed over for a living room. As the Shoreham pioneers demonstrated, there was ample scope for embellishment with some owners adding balconies and even towers. The community there attracted music hall celebrities and early film stars who came to make movies at the Shoreham studio built in 1913. Such people shunned the traditional seaside in favour of a more unconventional, do-it-yourself holiday experience. From Cumbria to Cornwall, train carriage bungalows were put up on isolated beaches until the 1930s. Forced wartime clearance saw the end of Shoreham's Bungalow Town but at places like East Wittering and Pagham Beach in Sussex or Sutton-on-Sea in Lincolnshire (previous page), the tell-tale carriage windows can still be seen on the sides of old holiday bungalows. ∎

Head-through Board

There cannot be many holidaymakers who have visited the seaside and *not* stuck their head through a hole in a board that transforms their body for the purpose of a funny photograph.

Whereas modern boards often have a nostalgic theme, perhaps putting twenty-first century heads on bodies dressed in old-fashioned bathing costumes, early scenes were much more varied.

By the 1890s the beach photographer had become a common sight, setting up his paraphernalia throughout the season to tempt visitors into posing for a shot to show people at home. With competition from multiple beach stalls, not to mention other photographers, the gimmick of a humorous head-through board rapidly gained ground. An 1891 newspaper article about Great Yarmouth commented that these were 'profusely displayed' on the sands, several taking well-known advertisements for their inspiration. Straplines used to sell Pears Soap had ample potential for innuendo when the words 'He won't be happy till he gets it' and 'You dirty boy!' were paired with a mismatch of faces and bodies.

Most photographers probably painted the boards themselves; some were made of canvas so they could simply be rolled up at the end of the day. Some designs were old favourites used year after year but others had a topicality which made them more short-lived. Collectors of this form of photograph can produce examples of Edwardians sitting in early motor cars, inter-war flapper girls in air ships and even people in mock television sets from the 1960s. The majority, however, relied on the humour of incongruity, old heads on young bodies and vice versa or the perennially popular gender swap. ◼

Some designs were old favourites used year after year but others had a topicality which made them more short-lived.

Boating Lake

For a long time seaside visitors had to share the beach
with working boats. Many boat owners diversified into giving
pleasure trips and it was a logical extension of this desire
among urban holidaymakers to play at being sailors,
that led to the creation of man-made boating lakes
along the seafront.

From the late-Victorian period land reclamation schemes opened up new space between defensive sea walls and existing buildings. At Southport visitors could avoid the long walk to the sea by hiring a boat on the vast Marine Lake created south of the pier in 1887. Around the same time, holidaymakers at Southsea in Hampshire were tempted to a new park built on reclaimed land at Eastney by the prospect of paddling a long wooden canoe on the aptly named Canoe Lake.

Between the wars another major phase of seafront expansion saw the growing proliferation of boating lakes, often dug out by unemployed labourers as a means

Boating Lake, Dovercourt Bay.

Between the wars another major phase of seafront expansion saw the growing proliferation of boating lakes

of Depression-era job creation. At Blackpool a semi-circular boating pool opened in 1923 as part of the new concrete promenade along North Shore. Other lakes took a more meandering form, notably the Venetian Waterways opened at Great Yarmouth in 1928 and the Skegness boating lake extended in 1930 to include a Venetian Bridge. Southport promoted its 'Venetian Night's' attraction suggesting an exotic carnival atmosphere, complete with illuminations and gondolas, centred on the new Venetian Bridge added to the Marine Lake in 1931. In all three cases the allure of the name was more important than any obvious design references to the Italian city. Dotted among the network of canals at Great Yarmouth, pictured on the previous page, were little shelters with thatched roofs while the electric-powered boats which toured the mile-long waterway were named after rivers on the nearby Norfolk broads.

By the 1950s almost every resort promenade had a boating lake and taking on the role of captain in an old-fashioned rowing boat, a swan-headed pedaloe or a miniature motor boat became an expected part of the post-war seaside holiday. ▪

Charabanc

The charabanc offered many British holidaymakers their first taste of motorised travel. As the precursor of today's coach, it was introduced from France in the early 1900s, becoming a common form of holiday transport after the First World War.

Effectively a long, open car the charabanc had rows of bench seats behind the driver, each with its own door, and a collapsible hood that could be pulled over passengers in inclement weather. Many ex-military lorries were converted into charabancs after 1918 and a railway strike the following year encouraged people to try new options for getting to the coast. In 1920 the press announced a charabanc 'Boom' as August Bank Holiday crowds took to the road in record numbers.

On the Saturday alone, some 10,000 people left Manchester by charabanc. Bridlington witnessed the arrival of fifty charabancs carrying more than 2,000 visitors, while at Scarborough travellers from Leeds accounted for thirty charabancs on their own. Seaside promenades were transformed by the presence of so many parked vehicles and it was evident the railway companies had genuine competition.

Vehicle design improved and as the interwar years progressed covered motor coaches began to supersede charabancs. People used the same name to describe both, often colloquially referring to them as 'charries', 'sharries' or 'chonkabonks'.

By 1937 approximately 40 million passenger journeys were made by charabanc and motor coach, split equally between the two. Unlike the railways, mass motor transport was classless. Though the coach took longer it was cheaper than the train and increasingly more comfortable than a third class rail carriage. For the first time people in rural areas who lacked a local rail connection could get easy access to the coast and charabancs also became popular for company outings and day trips organised by social clubs. As early as 1921 operators were advertising charabanc tours over several days to destinations beyond the big resorts. The era of greater holiday choice had begun. ■

By 1937 approximately 40 million passenger journeys were made by charabanc and motor coach, split equally between the two.

"I enjoyed what I saw 'coming down' by the Charabanc!"

Landlady

WE'VE COME TO THE END OF OUR HOLIDAY—
HOPE TO SEE YOU SOON.

Less of an object than a seaside institution,
the landlady was the butt of holidaymakers' jokes
from the music hall era well into the post war decades.

Comic postcards and end-of-the pier sketches portrayed a stereotypical battleaxe who ran her boarding house according to strict rules, charged for use of the cruet and required baths to be booked in advance.

No doubt there were landladies who conformed to this image but several factors should be considered in their defence. Whereas the manager of a hotel was likely to be male, apartments and boarding houses provided one of the few respectable employment options for widows and single women; wives also took in visitors to supplement their husbands' wages. Between 1897 and 1911, as Blackpool's staying clientele shifted from predominantly middle class to working class, the number of landladies increased tenfold from 400 to 4,000. Though the setting of their business was ostensibly domestic the unusual power they wielded over male guests could become a cause for resentment. Charging for extras was a symptom of having to make their annual income over the few short weeks of the summer season. During that time they worked extremely hard, choosing to keep visitors out between mealtimes so that they could undertake necessary housework and food preparation. Guests found this system increasingly out of tune with their expectations of a relaxing holiday but it was only with the growth of Bed and Breakfast accommodation from the 1950s that this began to change.

For all their bad press most landladies were honest and kind. To be otherwise was bad for business because satisfied customers often became repeat visitors, not to mention friends. When they joined together, landladies were a force to be reckoned with in resort politics. Now that the gendered division of labour is a thing of the past there are just as many seaside landlords as ladies. ▦

*For all their bad press
most landladies were
honest and kind.*

Fish and Chips

You haven't properly tasted fish and chips until
you've eaten it out of the paper, sitting on the beach
with sand gusting into your face.

Despite being a seaside staple, the historical evidence suggests that fish and chips began as a convenience food for the urban working classes. Jewish immigrants first introduced the idea of frying fish to England in the sixteenth century but it would take the combined new technologies of steam trawling, commercial ice-making and fast railway transport, to make fish a readily available food in Victorian London. By this time potatoes were also a street food in their own right though the idea of 'chipping' them came from either Belgium or France, both nations claiming the 'invention' of the chip for themselves.

Though it is impossible to say who first put the chip with the fried fish this certainly happened during the 1860s and a decade later the classic duo could be cheaply bought by working people in the street, in public houses, at fairs and increasingly in dedicated fish and chip shops. These began to appear at the seaside around the start of the twentieth century and by 1910 numbered around 25,000 nationwide. Most shops were small family-run businesses which were assisted, during the 1920s and 30s, by improvements in equipment for chipping and frying. Demand reached such an interwar peak that Margate could sustain the nation's biggest chippy; Picton's had restaurant seating for 700 holidaymakers. Contemporary comic postcards often featured fish and chips and the fact that it was such an easy, inexpensive takeaway for people to eat on the prom helped turn it into the quintessential seaside meal. Despite competition from a multitude of global fast foods, fish and chips still enjoys a special status in British cuisine and the smell of salt and vinegar is always that much tangier when it mingles with the briny sea air at holiday time. ▧

Most shops were small family-run businesses which were assisted, during the 1920s and 30s, by improvements in equipment for chipping and frying.

Railway Poster

In 1924 Sydney R. Jones declared that 'This is the day of the poster.'
Nowhere was this truer than for the nation's railways, amalgamated
the previous year from over 100 companies into the big four:
Great Western Railway, Southern Railway, London Midland
and Scottish Railway and London and North Eastern Railway.

Each developed its own advertising style that ensured station platforms were decorated with works by the leading poster artists of the day who proclaimed the joys of the seaside in seductive visual form.

Early railway posters were produced using letterpress until improvements in colour lithography allowed for the cheap creation of pictorial designs in the late Victorian era. These commonly took the form of a series of views which were too busy to be truly eye-catching. That changed after Frank Pick encouraged a more modern approach to posters on the London Underground and the national rail companies followed suit. The most innovative company was the LNER whose Advertising Manager, William Teasdale, put five top commercial artists under contract to the firm, selling their

posters to the public and even organising annual exhibitions of their work. Teasdale recognised the need for posters to convey their message quickly as passengers rushed past. Under his direction there was a new focus on beach scenes and images that depicted the fun of the seaside. A key example of this was the six poster series of 'East Coast Joys' designed by Tom Purvis, an artist who was acclaimed for his boldness and ability to reduce every subject to its simplest forms. The brightly coloured and strikingly stylised images produced for the railways through the 1920s and 30s now seem to encapsulate the spirit of the times.

Holiday traffic remained buoyant on the railways, in fact it tripled over the period, yet the actual share of total visitor numbers decreased as competition grew from motor coaches and cars. After the Second World War the nationalised railway continued to produce posters that lured people to the coast, the problem was that by the 1950s and 60s fewer of them were travelling there by train. ■

The brightly coloured and strikingly stylised images produced for the railways through the 1920s and 30s now seem to encapsulate the spirit of the times.

Bathing Belle

Almost as soon as it became acceptable for women to be seen in their bathing costumes the character of the Bathing Belle began to appear in promotional material for seaside resorts.

Used for posters, guidebook covers, hotel advertisements and postcards she epitomised the carefree days of summer. The suggestion she came from a place that attracted pretty girls ensured she had obvious appeal for male holidaymakers but her association with health and glamour was also designed to resonate with fellow women.

During the 1920s and 30s the message 'Come to Cromer, where the poppies grow', was combined on posters with a bathing belle sat on a sand dune with the sea to her left and the resort to her right. The famous red flowers of Poppyland sprinkled the grass, their colour heightened by the scarlet cloak draped around her shoulders. It proved such an enticing image that this bathing belle went through three different incarnations, always in the same pose but with updated swimwear and a progressively more modern

So powerful had the anonymous bathing belle become that she stood as a personification of the seaside itself.

graphic style. Through the interwar years Southern Railway's annual 'Hints for Holidays' publication also showed a marked preference for cover girls in swimwear though these women rarely showed their faces, either because they were transformed into Art Deco silhouettes or because they were depicted looking away from the reader towards the sea. So powerful had the anonymous bathing belle become that she stood as a personification of the seaside itself.

At the same time ordinary girls up and down the coast were taking part in beauty contests that sought to match real women to this idealised form. Such events became an expected part of the entertainment at open air pools and holiday camps from the Thirties well into the post-war era. Though feminist values have rightly challenged this kind of voyeurism most women took part willingly and, in an era when they were being liberated from the constraints of excessive clothing, the experience of a bathing belles parade must have felt thrillingly modern. ■

THE GUIDE TO CANVEY ISLAND

4D.

De la Warr Pavilion

The Sussex town of Bexhill-on-Sea was one of Edwardian England's most exclusive resorts. Besides its grand buildings, wealthy visitors were attracted by the opportunity to race their new motor cars along the seafront.

By the 1930s, however, fashions had changed and aristocratic tourists were heading for the Continent leaving the South Coast to the masses.

To revive Bexhill's reputation the landowner, 9th Earl De la Warr, announced an architectural competition for a new seafront venue in the 'International' style that was to offer a cutting edge mix of culture and entertainment. By choosing the émigré partnership of Russian Serge Chermayeff and German

Erich Mendelsohn, De la Warr's eponymous Pavilion became the most influential seaside building of its day and one which ranks among the greatest works of European Modernism.

The De la Warr Pavilion was constructed out of concrete and steel, with large glass windows, cantilevered balconies, clean lines and terrazzo floors. Inside, the 1,000-seat auditorium, restaurant, library, conference room and lounge offered a complementary vision of elegant interwar design. The crisp white exterior featured terraces for sunbathing and a rooftop sundeck where visitors could play quoits and other games fashionable on ocean liners. Costing £80,000, it opened on the 12 December 1935. The impact of its design was felt immediately as other seaside buildings referenced its iconic curved stair tower, most notably the new Winter Gardens at Ventnor on the Isle of Wight and Rothesay Pavilion on the Scottish Isle of Bute.

By the 1980s changing tastes and a lack of maintenance meant that the De la Warr Pavilion was in a poor state. Locals managed to get it designated in the top Grade I category of listed buildings and began seeking funds for its restoration. It re-opened following refurbishment in October 2005 and by its eightieth anniversary was welcoming 400,000 visitors a year to its art galleries and café bar. ■

Midland Hotel

The cream of interwar seaside visitors shunned existing grand hotels as too old-fashioned but there were attempts to woo the wealthy back with updated versions.

In 1933 the London, Midland and Scottish Railway commissioned architect Oliver Hill to design a replacement for their hotel at Morecambe. Responding to the curve of the promenade, Hill proposed a streamlined building three storeys high, with its entrance at the base of an elegant spiral staircase that rose through a central circular tower.

Boasting unrivalled views towards the Lakeland hills the Midland Hotel was strategically well placed within the LMS network, providing a natural place to break long journeys between the south and Scotland or the Isle of Man. For this reason the company was prepared to invest large sums of money on a team of top designers recruited by Hill.

The sculptor Eric Gill contributed two stylised seahorses to the outside of the staircase tower with a ceiling medallion inside depicting Neptune and Triton (opposite). He also created a wall map in the small South Room which puts the hotel at the heart of the North West region. Famed textile artist Marion Dorn designed two circular rugs for the entrance hall while painters Edward Bawden and Eric Ravilious were respectively employed to provide murals in the children's room and the café. Hill himself was preoccupied with fine details, ensuring that everything from grand pianos to bath plugs worked within his design scheme.

Artist Tirzah Garwood worked on the café murals with her husband Eric Ravilious and described in her diary how the opening day speeches on 12 July 1933

betrayed an uncertainty about the completed building; they 'were amusing in the sense that they almost openly said 'we don't like this hotel ourselves, but we hope to attract Americans with it.' In fact it was soon welcoming socialites from across the north of England and further afield. Though it certainly brought Morecambe a new caché the Midland Hotel lost its allure as fashions changed and in 1998 it was forced to close. After ten years of dereliction it was restored by developers Urban Splash and re-opened in 2008.

Responding to the curve of the promenade, Hill proposed a streamlined building three storeys high.

Beach Pyjamas

Between the wars legs became an accepted sight
on the beach and, thanks to a new fashion from France,
women's legs also became a talking point on the prom.

Nowhere else was the dress code relaxed enough for girls to wear trousers. Beach pyjamas, first worn by Coco Chanel, were adopted as *the* resort attire of Bright Young Things staying on the Riviera in the 1920s. With such glamorous associations they subsequently became a trend at the British seaside.

Named after the two-piece male pyjamas they emulated, the women's beach variety could be worn as a suit of loose fitting jacket and trousers but just as readily described the wide slacks worn on their own over a bathing costume. Made of vivid coloured cottons or *crêpe de Chine*, they were often printed with bright floral or geometric patterns. To complete the look beach pyjamas were combined with heels and floppy wide-brimmed hats.

'Le Pyjama' became such a phenomenon on the Cote d'Azur that a range of postcard views was produced depicting their wearers at resorts including Monte Carlo and Juan les Pins (left). In 1930s Britain postcards representing the trend were more likely to be the work of cartoonists poking fun. It didn't matter. The decadent hours of Riviera leisure were a long way from normal life as most people knew it and that was part of the attraction. Sporting beach pyjamas at Blackpool may not have been quite the same as wearing them at Cap 'dAntibes but it was a statement of increasing emancipation nonetheless. ▪

FUNNY TROUSERS SOME PEOPLE WEAR.

Made of vivid coloured cottons or crêpe de Chine, *they were often printed with bright floral or geometric patterns.*

Sporting beach pyjamas at Blackpool
may not have been quite the same as wearing them
at Cap 'dAntibes but it was a statement
of increasing emancipation nonetheless.

Walking Picture

Photographers took walking pictures on spec,
waiting at points along the promenade or pier
to snap people coming towards them.

The result was an unposed photo, taken before the subjects were aware of it and frequently captured mid-walk. With a receipt handed to them by the photographer,

holidaymakers could go and see their portrait later in the day after it had been developed into a postcard-sized print. As a form of seaside souvenir the 'walkie' was extremely popular from the 1920s, falling out of favour as camera ownership became the norm.

It was not just the holidaymakers who walked. Photographers themselves were employed to be mobile and during their daily walks would take hundreds of snapshots of people sitting on the sand, relaxing outside their beach hut or paddling in the sea. After the war some photographers used props in the shape of large stuffed animals, getting children to pose with donkeys or unrealistic-looking lions and tigers. Group shots of families or work colleagues were good for business because the finished photograph had the potential to sell multiple copies. In the early days, when glass plate negatives were used, a reference number would be scratched onto the plate itself explaining the scrawls still visible in many surviving photos. This number then had to be found among thousands of pictures pinned up on boards outside the photographer's kiosk. From the late-1930s Wrates' Snaps sold their walking pictures for 1s. each from a shop at the entrance to Skegness pier, the access ramps to which were cluttered with fifteen or more such photo boards. Sunbeam of Margate was one of the biggest seaside operators with branches at Westgate, Cliftonville, Broadstairs and Ramsgate. At the height of their business activities, Sunbeam employed 300 seasonal staff and on a busy Bank Holiday before the war their photographers could take up to 35,000 walking images. ▪

*At the height of their business activities,
Sunbeam employed 300 seasonal staff and on a busy
Bank Holiday before the war their photographers
could take up to 35,000 walking images.*

Amusement Arcade

Barron's Paradium of 1919 can lay claim to being
the first purpose-built amusement arcade in Britain.

Located on Marine Parade in Great Yarmouth, it developed from the 1897 Jubilee Exhibition where the Barron brothers installed What the Butler Saw machines to complement the early cinematograph films they were showing.

The brothers subsequently went into business manufacturing coin-operated 'automatic' machines and decided to give these their own dedicated premises.

Over the next two decades the slot machine industry developed rapidly

This 1950s arcade at Jaywick in Essex used bold signage. Today bright lights are a must.

with arcades opening around the coast. In the 1920s holidaymakers could visit Clacton pier's Crystal Casino Amusement Arcade or the Palace of Fun on Brighton Palace Pier, housed in the former theatre. Blaring music was a feature from the start, a report on the seafront Palace of Fun at Hastings describing how 'a very fine installation of loud speakers connected with the wireless and a gramophone is in constant use, [and] adds materially to the enjoyment of all.'

In the myriad amusement centres along Blackpool's Golden Mile the interwar favourites were competitive football games designed for two players. Another popular penny-in-the-slot machine was the German-made Clucking Hen, that laid colourful metal eggs with a trinket inside; until Hitler transferred production to the war effort British arcades were being supplied with 5 million eggs a year.

Other 1930s machines updated the tradition of seaside fortune-telling with printed cards delivered by such technological marvels as The Robot King, The Radio Analyst and The Green Ray Television Wonder. Precursors of modern fruit machines were in evidence as were pinball machines and prize cuddly toys.

By the 1960s pier arcades were common everywhere with the newest American import of Bingo finding a place in many of them. The subsequent popularity of video games spelled the end for surviving penny machines as Space Invaders gave way to the massive success of Japanese import Pac Man in 1980. Today most arcade games use digital technology but there is still a place for the old fashioned penny rollers that hold out the prospect of a big win if you can *just* knock that one tuppence off its ledge. ◾

Palm Tree

TORQUAY
THE ENGLISH RIVIERA

Exotic vegetation has long been used to help the seaside feel like a place apart from ordinary life and the palm tree encapsulates that idea better than anything else.

It was used as a key decorative motif in the interiors of Brighton's Royal Pavilion and featured in the displays of fauna that filled Victorian winter gardens.

From the early twentieth century hardy varieties were imported and cultivated for outdoor use, particularly in the milder resorts of south west England that promoted themselves as Riviera destinations.

Though palms were not native to the French Riviera, by the time British socialites discovered the beaches around Nice in the 1920s tropical plants, such as the *Phoenix canariensis* introduced in 1864, had become an established part of the landscape. Their use in south Devon and Cornwall was a very conscious effort by resort authorities to draw parallels with the sunshine and glamour of the Mediterranean coast. More than any other town, Torquay used the palm as a symbol of its status as 'Queen of the English Riviera'. Sun soaked depictions of its palm-tree-lined promenades were used to sell the resort as a

More than any other town, Torquay used the palm as a symbol of its status as 'Queen of the English Riviera'.

year-round destination, lending it an air of foreign luxury and elegance. Interwar railway posters were dominated by foreground palm trees, relegating other attractions to the background. In 1982 this idea was taken to its logical conclusion by graphic artist John Gorman who produced a striking image of a single silhouetted palm against three blocks of colour that denoted blue sky, green sea and yellow sand. It remains an iconic vision of the English Riviera. ▪

Sun Tan Lotion

The first commercial preparations against sun burn were formulated in the 1930s. Natural remedies using plant extracts, oil and minerals had a long history of use going back to early civilizations but the mass uptake of sunbathing created a new market for synthetic products.

Eugene Schueller, the founder of cosmetics brand L'Oreàl, set his chemists to the task of inventing a remedy to protect his fair skin whilst he was sailing on the French Riviera. In April 1935 they gave him 'sun oil' which used benzyl solicylate as its active ingredient to absorb the UVB light responsible for burning the skin. Two months later Schueller launched this product under the trade name Ambre Solaire.

Just like sea bathing before it, sunbathing developed from medical origins. German and Swiss pioneers extolled the virtues of sunshine from the turn of the twentieth century, with particular emphasis on the treatment of tuberculosis and rickets. Then, in 1923, Coco Chanel arrived by yacht at Cannes 'brown as a cabin boy'. She did not 'invent' sunbathing but she made having a tan exquisitely fashionable.

In the Holiday Supplement of *Everywoman's Magazine* for July 1937 Boots the Chemist promoted sun tan oil to induce 'that Riviera appearance!' For those who burnt rather than tanned there was Witch Hazel sunburn lotion for the same 1 shilling price. Whereas these products were not designed to protect the skin, Nurona Sunbronze Cream promised a 'tan

In 1923, Coco Chanel arrived by yacht at Cannes 'brown as a cabin boy'. She did not 'invent' sunbathing but she made having a tan exquisitely fashionable.

without tears'. This early British sunscreen was in production by 1939, manufactured by Manchester chemists James Woolley, Sons & Co. After the war Coppertone went on sale in America and Piz Buin was launched on the Continent by Austrian chemist Franz Greiter, its name taken from the Piz Buin alpine peak where he had suffered painful sunburn as a student climber in 1937. It was Greiter who introduced the concept of Sun Protection Factor or SPF during the 1960s. This calculation about how long a person can be exposed to the sun wearing sunscreen took on greater significance as research in the 1970s began to demonstrate the link between UV rays and skin cancer. Today the market for sun tan lotion is worth billions. ▧

Devon Blue

When the First World War came the import of German
souvenirs stopped. This left a lucrative market
to be filled at the end of hostilities.

One of the products to fill this gap was 'Devon Blue', defined by its colour and made by a group of potteries around Torquay and Bovey Tracey. Eschewing the Victorian transfer print, its only decoration was provided by the name of a tourist site, inland or coastal, usually scratched into the glaze.

Whereas earlier souvenir china had tended to be based upon thin, white porcelain, Devon Blue had a much sturdier feel reflecting the fact that it came from former Art Potteries. The late nineteenth century interior design trend for 'Art at Home' placed new emphasis on craftsmanship meaning that small potteries could charge a premium for their handmade wares and sell to people who self-consciously shunned mass-produced factory goods. By the 1920s things had moved on and to stay in business companies like Devonmoor began churning out simple designs for the souvenir trade. Reflecting the fashions of the time handles of teapots, jugs and mugs often had an angular shape suggestive of Art Deco without being too modern that it put off purchasers with more conservative tastes.

Devon Blue was perfect for the 'cheap and cheerful' holiday market and it was common for seaside visitors to buy a piece wherever they went. Production stopped in the early 1980s but vintage examples can still be had for very little money. They belong to the twentieth century heyday of the British seaside holiday, in a deep blue that speaks of the sea and sky along the English Rivieria just a short distance away from the potteries where they were made. ■

Holiday Camp Chalet

During the 1930s holiday camps were hailed as a revolution in seaside accommodation. For their all-inclusive fee guests got access to a host of sports and entertainments combined with a level of comfort unachievable in conventional tent camping.

When Britain's first holiday camp opened on the Isle of Man in 1894, its male campers slept in round bell tents, twelve pairs of feet pointing to the centre with heads around the edge like the spokes of a wheel. This arrangement helped foster an important camaraderie or 'camp spirit' but as holiday camps developed into more commercial ventures after the First World War the standards of sleeping accommodation rose.

The new type of permanent chalets were typically timber, laid out in rows that promoted neighbourliness whilst also allowing for a rare degree of privacy. Getting their own chalet key upon arrival at camp meant that holidaymakers could access their little home-from-home whenever they wished. This was a big contrast to the seaside boarding house where the front door key remained firmly in the landlady's possession.

Chalet furnishings were simple; single, double or bunk beds,

clothes storage, a chair and a wash basin with cold tap. Toilets and baths were in communal blocks. The first *ensuite* bathrooms appeared in the 1950s as the basic pitched roof chalet began to be upgraded to suit changing tastes. Self-catering units were introduced onto renamed holiday 'centres' from the 1960s and though chalets lived on they did so as the cheapest form of seaside accommodation. The 1930s chalets pictured opposite survive at Brighstone on the Isle of Wight and the last original Butlin's chalet is now a listed building. After a long period of being deeply unfashionable, deluxe modernised chalets were re-introduced to Butlin's Minehead resort in 2015. ■

Butlin's Redcoat

In 1936 Billy Butlin began his mission to transform
the traditional seaside holiday. Having made a fortune from
his chain of coastal amusement parks he invested everything he had
in a new type of holiday camp, designed to provide affordable
luxury for middle income guests.

His plan relied upon making a small profit from a large number of people. This approach would allow him to offer a wider range of facilities than any of his competitors. Effectively, it meant building an entirely self-contained resort outside the Lincolnshire town of Skegness, where access to everything – accommodation, food and entertainment – was included in a one-off weekly charge.

The first visitors to arrive at Butlin's were met with large Modern-style dining halls and bars, chalets stretching in rows towards the sea and a multitude of sporting options that included tennis, swimming, bowls and physical training classes. Despite this abundance Billy Butlin noticed that his guests were looking bored as they wandered aimlessly around the site. Unused to things being free, people were unsure of the etiquette and reticent to ask fellow holidaymakers. They needed someone to break the ice, to invite them to participate and create a friendly atmosphere. Within a week the Butlin's Redcoat had been born.

The trademark scarlet blazer, with a 'B' embroidered on the pocket, made it immediately clear to campers that these were staff members paid to help. Their presence ensured that the massive sites always had a strong community feel despite being occupied by a new group of people every week. By 1946, when the Skegness camp could accommodate 4,500 guests, there was one Redcoat for every twenty-five campers. So visible were the Redcoats that they became celebrities on camp; some even became household names off it, including Des O'Connor, Jimmy Tarbuck, Johnny Ball and Stephen Mulhern. Rival holiday camp chains Warner's and Pontin's had green and blue coats respectively. More than eighty years after their introduction the Redcoats remain at the core of Butlin's identity as a seaside holiday company. ■

Ocean Liner Architecture

It was never long before the holiday habits
of the rich and famous spawned more accessible
versions on the British coast.

With construction of Cunard's luxury flagship RMS Queen Mary cruising became a key influence and in the wake of her maiden voyage in May 1936 a number of seaside buildings were designed in imitation ocean liner style. The largest was Marine Court, at St Leonard's-on-Sea in Sussex. Billed as a 'Luxury Liner on Land', it was Britain's tallest residential building when it opened in 1938, boasting over a hundred flats with balconies shaped to look like the bridge of a ship (right). In case the allusion was not clear enough Cunard-White Star Line lent a 24 foot long model of their latest vessel for display inside the main entrance.

Holiday camps also employed the ocean liner aesthetic. The Clipper Bar at Prestatyn Holiday Camp had a rounded prow overlooking the open air pool with a wheel house on its flat sun roof complete with mast. Another 1939 camp was Middleton Tower near Morecambe which adopted the promotional catchphrase of 'cruising on land'. Not only were its main buildings constructed to look like liners, '...To add to the nautical effect, panelling and furnishings from the luxury liners Berengeria and Leviathan have been used for the sun lounge, palm court, ballroom and banquet hall'. Berengeria had once been the largest passenger vessel in the world so reusing its old fixtures and fittings added a true trans-Atlantic glamour.

At Blackpool Pleasure Beach architect Joseph Emberton gave his Casino, pictured opposite, an eye-catching spiral tower, behind

Marine Court, St. Leonards-on-Sea.

Billed as a 'Luxury Liner on Land', it was Britain's tallest residential building when it opened in 1938, boasting over a hundred flats with balconies shaped to look like the bridge of a ship.

which he designed a rounded concrete building with two upper decks of glazing topped off by a red and black funnel. Such architectural devices drew explicit parallels with the 'floating palaces' enjoyed by the social elite. They worked at the seaside because ordinary people standing on deck could look out to sea and imagine themselves sailing off into the distance. ■

Lido

Lidos epitomised the interwar trend
for healthy exercise in the fresh air.

They took their name from the Venice Lido resort with its connotations of Continental sunshine and luxurious glamour. Between 1930 and 1939, at least 180 open air swimming pools were built in Britain; the biggest and most expensive were to be found at the seaside.

Construction began on the first coastal lido in 1914 when work on strengthening the sea wall of Scarborough's South Bay incorporated a pool to provide safe bathing in all tidal conditions. The council owners soon found they could generate significant new income from galas and water carnivals, a fact which explains why the Blackpool Open Air Baths of 1923 featured seating for 3,000 spectators. Even on a normal summer's day the number of people watching outstripped those in the water and only 94,403 of the half million people who paid for entry in Blackpool's first full season, were actually bathers.

Competition between resorts was intense and the scale of lido building reflected this. In 1933 Hastings and St Leonards attempted to enter the big league with a vast concrete bathing pool that also featured a gymnasium, sun terrace and underground car park. A year later New Brighton Bathing Pool opened with swanky Art Deco buildings ringing a seafront site of more than 4 acres. The apex came with Morecambe's aptly named Super Swimming Stadium opened in July 1936 at a cost of £130,000. Few resorts failed to build an

outdoor pool. Clacton's was noteworthy for being the only example on a pier while Weston-super-Mare became famous for its beautifully cantilevered diving stage. Most satisfyingly Modern was the relatively small example of Saltdean Lido near Brighton, with a two storey building that embraced the pool in its curved concrete arms. In 1987, Saltdean was the first lido to be listed; many others had already been lost, unsustainable in the British climate once the fashion wore off. Two key exceptions both date from 1935. Plymouth's Tinside Lido and the Jubilee Pool at Penzance continue to welcome swimmers following major conservation work. Plans for the full restoration of Saltdean Lido are ongoing. ▪

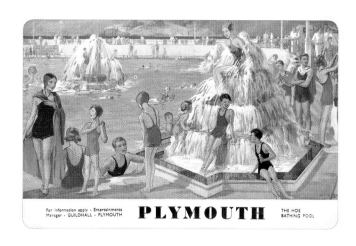

For Information apply · Entertainments Manager · GUILDHALL · PLYMOUTH **PLYMOUTH** THE HOE BATHING POOL

Art Deco
Bathing Costume

By 1914 the acceptance of mixed bathing had wrought important changes in the status of the bathing costume.

Now a more visible item of apparel, moves were afoot to give it a more flattering shape which would not be too revealing when wet. As surviving photographs show, these goals were not always achievable with the materials at hand but that began to change from the 1920s.

During that decade the ratio of bare skin to bathing costume shifted for both sexes. Year by year the amount of fabric diminished as a more recognisably modern form emerged. The one-piece suit was now made of figure-hugging machine-knitted wool, with shoulder straps instead of sleeves, increasingly low cut at the back and with the sides scooped out to help maximise tan-ability. Women's styles reflected the androgynous silhouette of the flapper employing abstract Art Deco patterns to enhance a new, more athletic look. In 1929 Jantzen promoted their latest model as 'the suit than changed bathing into swimming.'

In the 1930s new materials took the bathing costume forward.

The Dunlop rubber company invented a very fine elastic yarn made from latex rubber covered with thread which they launched as Lastex in 1931. Since Lastex did not bag or sag when wet, strappy designs were able to hold their shape even after a dip and ever more revealing styles were brought to market. Around this time young men ditched the top of their costumes and bathed in high waisted trunks, often worn with a belt. ■

Ice Cream Parlour

Knicker Bocker Glory. Peach Melba. Banana Split.
The very names conjure up that brand of Italian ice cream
parlour that began to appear at the seaside during the 1930s.

Street sellers from southern Italy, many of whom had first settled in Scotland, spread out around the coast offering their home-made ice cream in a new range of sundaes and *parfaits* served in specially designed glasses amid fashionable Art Deco surroundings.

The inspiration came from America where ice cream parlours had spread rapidly during the Prohibition era. In Britain they represented a glamorous import with similar appeal to Hollywood movies, cocktails and jazz. Among the iced inventions on offer were the Come Along Sundae, Aviation Glide, Ting-a-ling and Lavender Lady.

Today the enduring favourites continue to be served by younger generations of ice cream dynasties, as at Notarianni's in Blackpool (established 1928), Morelli's at Broadstairs (opened 1932) and Brucciani's at Morecambe (opened 1939). Many of the pioneers were related to each other so the Morelli's branched out to Northern Irish resorts, members of the Rossi clan had parlours in Southend and Weymouth, and Pacittos sold their trademark 'Lemon tops' in Redcar and Scarborough (opposite). In 1952 the Notarianni family of Blackpool and the Vettesse family of Great Yarmouth were joined by marriage.

Though they are increasingly rare, ice cream parlours with early décor give an extra vintage flavour to the eating experience. Morelli's still announces its presence with a flying canopy and neon signage installed in 1959; the pink leatherette seating and Lloyd Loom chairs inside the Broadstairs parlour are of the same date. At Scarborough's Harbour Bar the Alonzi family have kept their 1950s signage and red-and-yellow colour scheme sticking to formica and vinyl for the counters, tabletops and banquettes. At Notarianni's in Eastbourne they even have the old fake sundaes in the window that were used to display the choice of ice creams on offer some fifty years ago. Sadly the neon extravaganza pictured below at Peppinos, Great Yarmouth was lost to fire in 2008. ▨

In Britain they represented a glamorous import with similar appeal to Hollywood movies, cocktails and jazz.

Dance Hall

As dancing became an increasingly popular holiday pastime the venues to accommodate it grew bigger and grander. Their lavish design was emphasised in names like The Palace at Douglas and the Queen's Palace at Rhyl.

At Blackpool, the Tower Ballroom set the standard for them all (opposite). In 1899 it became one of the first places in the country to install a sprung floor that bounced gently as dancers moved across it. Though this innovation was crucial in making it more comfortable to dance for long periods of time, holidaymakers also enjoyed the novelty of open-air dancing on piers.

After the First World War people fell in love with dancing like never before. The imported music of American ragtime and jazz bought with it the big band sound and the promise of much greater physical contact between the sexes. In the 1920s foxtrots and quicksteps replaced the old fashioned sequence dances and polkas. Pier pavilions and roller skating rinks were converted into seaside dance halls with yet more being purpose-built. In 1923 *The Brighton Herald* reported from the recently opened Regent Dance Hall atop the Regent Cinema: 'To enter without preparation into that great new hall...is to get the effect of a rocket bursting in one's face. The hall is like an explosion of all the primary and secondary colours, flung hither and thither in a restless, intersecting criss-cross of blazing light'. A happy buzz rose from the floor, mixing live music with the chat of 'sitters out' and 'balcony watchers'.

Holiday camps had dance halls; soon every urban high street had them, catering to the increased leisure time of ordinary working people well into the 1960s. After that, recorded music superseded live bands and women no longer waited to be asked to dance, taking to the floor solo for dances like the twist. Those dance halls that did not close altogether were replaced by discos, nightclubs or bingo. ▪

Crazy Golf

Golf has a long history in Scotland but one of the earliest
English courses was by the sea at Westward Ho!
where the Royal North Devon Club was established in 1864.

The game grew in popularity over the next fifty years until, in September 1922, the Prince of Wales (later Duke of Windsor) teed off at St Andrews and sparked a nationwide fashion for the game, along with its eccentric uniform of 'plus fours', or baggy tweed knickerbockers. Resorts created putting greens to capitalise on the trend. Rothesay had one on its Esplanade by 1924 and Brighton got its miniature golf links by the West Pier a couple of years later.

The next big thing was crazy golf. As early as 1907, British army colonel William Senhouse Clarke, had patented 'Gofstacle', a blend of golf and croquet that featured obstacles including hoops, rings, tunnels and bridges. It took the Americans to realise the potential of his idea. Such was the US craze for crazy golf that in the late 1920s courses were built for office workers on the top of skyscrapers. In 1930 the first National Tom Thumb Championship was played near Chattanooga on a course where every hole was themed on a different fairytale. That summer 4 million Americans played daily and cinemas reported a slump in takings as customers transferred their business to all-night crazy golf courses.

In Britain the new game was marketed as 'golf for the masses'. Skegness had a fifteen-hole crazy golf course in 1927, which may have been the nation's first, but they quickly sprang up around the coast. In 1931 an indoor midget golf course was installed on Brighton Palace Pier designed to take players on 'A Drive Through London' (pun intended). A second phase of interest occurred in the 1960s when the introduction of new materials such as fibreglass permitted even crazier landscapes. Today players at Cleethorpes can negotiate a miniature version of the pier pavilion in sight of the real building while Weymouth actually has a crazy golf course on its beach. ■

Weymouth actually has a crazy golf course on its beach.

Barbed Wire

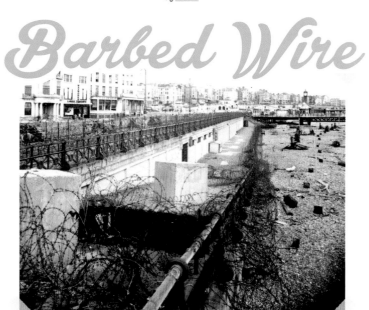

When war broke out in 1939 England's beaches
suddenly became the front line in the nation's fight
against Nazi Germany. Invasion fears led to the creation of an
exclusion zone covering the coast, and a considerable strip of land
behind it, from The Wash in Norfolk to Lyme Regis in Dorset.

Manned checkpoints controlled access as resorts welcomed soldiers and civil servants in place of holidaymakers.

Barbed wire obstacles were one of the first defences to be placed on beaches from May 1940. Just above high water mark and parallel to the sea, coils of concertina wire were combined with 'double apron' fences that were difficult to cut or climb. Beaches were mined while seafronts were equipped with pillboxes, gun emplacements and

"Look what I've found, Mummie!"

concrete battlements. German intelligence officers used pre-war seaside postcards to inform their invasion plans so the British government was right to worry about the potential for piers to be used as convenient landing stages. In summer 1940 orders were given for fifty three piers to be requisitioned in order that sections of decking could be removed with immediate effect. Though all were handed back by late 1944 some would never re-open.

Many south and east coast resorts suffered hit and run attacks by enemy aircraft. Margate was hit by more than 2,700 bombs and shells destroying 238 buildings and damaging nearly 9,000 others. When a journalist from *The Times* visited in August 1943 he found that 'from being a bright and well-kept background to cheerful holidaymaking, Margate has become damaged and shabby.' Just two hotels were open for business compared to the pre-war number of 240. In the North West things were very different. Blackpool was too far away to be actively under threat and it enjoyed unprecedented prosperity during the war thanks to service personnel, munitions workers and free-spending Americans from Warton air base. When peace finally came and the barbed wire was removed from Britain's beaches, the pent up demand for seaside holidays led to record visitor numbers. On the last Saturday of July 1945 102,889 rail passengers steamed into Blackpool alone. ▪

Knitted Swimsuit

The childhood memory of sagging wet wool is shared
by many members of the postwar Baby Boom generation,
who first experienced the sea dressed in a knitted swimsuit.

Such costumes, which seemed to go on for years as they stretched to fit their wearers, were typical beach attire for children until the mid-1950s.

By the end of the Second World War Britons were desperate to get back to the seaside and for the first time it became feasible for the mass of ordinary working people to

Magazines such as Stitchcraft provided attractive patterns for knitted bathing costumes aimed at all members of the family.

relatively few working class children were seen at the beach. The 1938 Holidays with Pay Act changed that but its full impact was not felt until after 1945 when 11 million more people were finally able to take advantage of paid annual leave. Unfortunately clothes rationing remained in force for a further four years, which meant mothers had to be creative about providing their children with swimwear. After years of following the wartime mantra of Make Do and Mend British women were more than up to the task and magazines such as *Stitchcraft* provided attractive patterns for knitted bathing costumes aimed at all members of the family, including father.

As times improved shops began to carry a greater range of children's swimsuits and the home-made variety looked increasingly old fashioned. For little girls the most desirable costumes were made of an elasticated fabric ruched around the body and secured with a tie at the neck. Though these also had a tendency to concertina-down in the water and collect sand in the ruches they were definitely a step up from the home knit which belongs to a very particular moment in our seaside history.

take their children for more than a day trip. In previous decades the expense of staying away from home when a week off work meant a week without wages ensured that

Barrow Boys

Holidaymakers arriving by coach or train were met
at the seaside by groups of young boys all calling out
'barrow for your luggage, sir?'

From the interwar years to the mid-1980s lads who lived on the coast performed a valuable service walking visitors to their accommodation whilst conveying their heavy suitcases on homemade barrows and providing information about shows and local attractions.

The typical starting age was ten or eleven. Every Saturday during the summer season barrow boys rose early to meet the first wave of visitors descending on resorts. Between 7am and 4pm they could walk miles from station to guesthouse and back again. The generosity of most holidaymakers made it worthwhile. Boys quickly learnt that having a set rate was less lucrative than leaving it up to the customer to decide. In the mid-1960s a good day's 'luggaging' could yield up to £10 and many a barrow boy bought his first bike on the proceeds. Once dropped off, visitors often booked the same boy to take them back to the station one or two Saturdays later. Some boys even managed to earn commission from guesthouse owners if they took people who had not booked accommodation in advance. Holiday camps used barrow boys too, giving the select few official passes or company caps.

Some former barrow boys recall battles with older boys for the best pitch and animosity from taxi drivers who disliked the competition. Most have happy memories of the companionship among their informal workforce. The barrows themselves came in all shapes and sizes depending on the DIY skill of older male relations. Pram wheels and scrap wood were the main component parts. The canniest boys found ways to fix barrows on to their bikes to hasten their return to the station. One boy at Great Yarmouth apparently made twice as much as his competitors by having a 'barra' with carpet on the top so as not to scratch the suitcases and a waterproof cover stowed in a lockable box for use on rainy days! ▪

Boys quickly learnt that having a set rate was less lucrative than leaving it up to the customer to decide.

Sea Wall

I am your Sea Wall
I stand here 24.7.365
No matter how high the tide
Or how strong the wind
You can depend on me
And sleep safely at night
But it has not always been so
This is my story.....

The Beginning

2 NORMA AND DAVID MERRICK ?
FRIENDS OF CONCORD BEACH

Over the last two centuries seaside resorts have invested huge sums of money in replacing the irregular, natural form of the coastline with rigid, unchanging sea walls.

Stone structures from the Victorian era have given way to expanses of twentieth century concrete but the goal is the same; to defend the man-made seaside against the force of the sea and the threat of coastal erosion.

At Canvey Island in Essex the sea wall rises high above the heads of promenaders who can only access the shore via steps through this concrete barricade. A sea view is less important here than the sense of protection afforded by the wall. The murals shown here were painted at Concord Beach in 2014 and vividly illustrate how crucial the wall is to ensuring the safety of people and property on the low-lying land behind. On 31 January 1953 existing sea defences were breached by an unprecedented storm surge that killed fifty eight people and led to the island's evacuation.

Right along England's east coast, communities suffered as abnormally strong winds blew off the Arctic circle at the same time as the Spring tide rose some eight feet above predicted levels. In 1953 there was no warning system in place to alert residents of the coming storm which had a particularly devastating effect on communities with large numbers of insubstantial holiday bungalows, built on land below sea level. At Sutton-on-Sea in Lincolnshire, 900,000 tons of sand and water washed into the streets killing forty-three people; at the interwar bungalow resort of Jaywick in Essex, thirty five people lost their lives. The overall death toll for England was 307. ■

At Canvey Island a sea view is less important than the sense of protection offered by the sea wall.

Residents were taken unawares of the flooding

THE ROGERS FAMILY
FRIENDS OF CONCORD BEACH

Beach Hut

The first purpose-built beach huts appeared in the 1890s as holidaymakers began to challenge the dominance of bathing machines.

Mobile changing rooms were no longer necessary when it was socially acceptable for people to walk to the sea in their bathing costumes so whole fleets of machines had their wheels taken off to be parked at the top of the beach. This change in use marked an important turning point. Canvas tents and municipal 'bathing bungalows' began to be provided

at Edwardian resorts to supply visitors with a little home-from-home. Unlike bathing machines, which had only ever been let on a 'per dip' basis, these were available for extended hire periods.

Between the wars the number of beach huts increased peaking, along with visitor numbers, in the 1950s and 60s. As foreign sunshine lured people away from the British coast

Huts can be built on stilts like those pictured left at Wells-next-the-Sea, or in formation like at Hayling Island to the right.

they fell from favour until, in the late 1990s, press reports revealed a resurgent interest as beach huts started selling for inflated prices at hot spots including Southwold, Whitstable, Wells-next-the-Sea and Mudeford.

Their popularity has always been based on the convenience of having somewhere private to change where all the paraphernalia of a day at the beach can be stored and a cup of tea brewed. Huts rarely have mains drainage, water, gas or electricity but occupants find ways around this; some clever cooks can even muster a full Sunday roast in their beach hut by relying on bottled gas. Where council bye-laws allow, the huts present a rainbow of colour ways but even at beaches where the range of tones is prescribed owners manage to personalise their space with cherished names.

Demand now so outstrips supply that a number of local authorities have put beach huts at the centre of coastal regeneration projects. The first to do this was East Lindsey District Council which launched Bathing Beauties in 2006, an international design competition to re-imagine the beach hut for the twenty-first century. The winning designs were built at Mablethorpe and Sutton-on-Sea. Notwithstanding such new adaptations it is the humble shed on the seashore that has become a seaside icon, a position it looks set to hold for the foreseeable future. ■

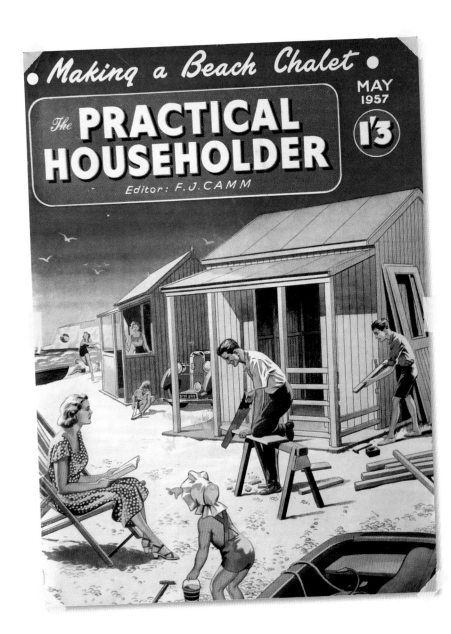

Making a Beach Chalet

MAY
1957

The PRACTICAL
HOUSEHOLDER

Editor: F.J. CAMM

1'3

Seafood Stall

Shellfish makes the obvious seaside snack
and generations have eaten it standing up
at a stall or sitting on the beach.

Victorian beach pedlars
sold shrimp in little pointed calico
bags while oyster vendors carried
'a round basket, a bottle of vinegar
and a dirty towel for wiping

customer's hands.' Until the end
of the nineteenth century shrimps
were the more prestigious of the
two and potted shrimps, flavoured
with nutmeg and preserved under
a crust of butter, were a real

seaside treat. At Morecambe the Baxter family have been producing this delicacy for over 200 years. Oysters, on the other hand, were as cheap and plentiful as whelks and winkles, bought by trippers and gulped down by the dozen. One of Blackpool Promenade's oldest surviving buildings is Robert's Oyster Rooms, set up by John Roberts of Preston in 1876. His customers could enjoy seven oysters for a shilling but had to supply their own black velvet – a mix of stout and champagne – to wash them down. The business is still going but these days the oysters are rather more expensive. Now representing the posh end of seafood they have their own festival at Whitstable every July.

As seafood stalls migrated from the beach their colourful displays and signage became a distinctive element of the promenade. In 1951 artist Barbara Jones wrote glowingly about the whelk stalls she found at Brighton. Behind the little white plates set with individual helpings of mussels, jellied eels, whelks, pink shrimps and black winkles many of the stall holders used bright green artificial grass instead of table cloths. When the carefully placed vinegar, salt and pepper were taken into account she concluded that 'No exclusive restaurant ever had its side tables more alluringly garnished than a good whelk stall.' There was no faster food; 'the visitor, who really is not hungry at all, has only to pay a copper or two, pick up his saucer, shake on a dash of this or that, and eat it all effortlessly with a little wooden spoon.' ▧

Oysters were as cheap and plentiful as whelks and winkles, bought by trippers and gulped down by the dozen.

Kiss Me Quick Hat

Souvenirs come and go but the Kiss Me Quick hat
has enjoyed a surprising longevity.

Seaside shops began selling felt cowboy hats in the 1950s when the Lone Ranger was at the height of his fame.

Ribbons with slogans began to appear around the crown in the following decade when the most likely origin of the 'Kiss Me Quick' phrase was the 1961 song of the same name by Elvis Presley. Another phrase that made its way onto hats was the anti-Vietnam slogan 'Make love not War'.

These hats were only ever meant to be worn at the seaside following a tradition that saw 1930s excursionists sporting the cotton hats of sailors and went on to incorporate Spanish sombreros later in the Sixties. They were examples of holiday attire bought for wearing on the prom, that were put away as soon as people got home. The Kiss Me Quick hat became a favourite because it had just the right amount of sauciness, no doubt being used as an ice-breaker by young men hoping for some action under the pier.

By the end of the twentieth century it had been adopted by hen parties, now available from seaside retailers in the form of candyfloss pink Stetsons trimmed with feathers. The phrase itself has become synonymous with a particular type of seaside culture and is often used in a pejorative way to describe the tackier side of big resorts. If it is not to everyone's taste the Kiss Me Quick seaside nevertheless reflects a permissive, escapist atmosphere that can be traced back to the eighteenth century and the Prince Regent himself. ■

The most likely origin of the 'Kiss Me Quick' phrase was the 1961 song of the same name by Elvis Presley.

Bikini

Although the exposure of female flesh became acceptable
during the interwar decades the 1946 launch of the Bikini
proved that there was still a limit.

An unwritten rule had previously kept the navel covered up; revealing it turned out to be highly controversial.

Mosaics discovered at the Villa Romana del Casala in Sicily reveal that women wore bikini-type costumes when exercising around 300AD. It took until the 1930s for the two-piece to come back into fashion. During the Second World War exposing the midriff meant saving valuable fabric but knickers were always high-waisted. The race to challenge convention happened in France where two designers launched new smaller costumes within months of each other. In May 1946 Jacques Heim, owner of a beach shop at Cannes, introduced his minimalist 'Atome' named after the smallest known particle of matter. Whereas his design just covered the navel that of Louis Réard, an engineer whose mother owned a Parisian lingerie boutique, entirely dispensed with that nicety. Réard used just 30 square inches of fabric cut into four squares and took the name of 'Bikini' as the atomic bomb tests at Bikini atoll happened just four days before he went public. Both Heim and Réard explicitly associated their products with modernity; it took the rest of the world some time to catch up.

Popular culture finally embraced the bikini in the 1960s with significant help from Brian Hyland's 1960 song 'Itsy Bitsy Teeny Weeny Yellow Polka Dot Bikini' and *that* scene in the 1962 Bond film 'Dr No' when Ursula Andress emerged from the sea in a white bikini accessorized with a knife. An expression of the era's sexual revolution, the bikini was now widely available; Debenhams department store carried boldly patterned Bri-Nylon for the 1965 season while the trend for crochet meant girls could also make their own. Resort publicity now actively featured bikinis to show how 'with it' seaside towns were. Fears about skin cancer led to a dip in popularity during the 1990s but today the bikini outsells all other beach wear. ■

An expression of the era's sexual revolution, the bikini was now widely available.

Surfboard

The iconic shape of the modern surfboard has come to stand for an alternative beach culture that developed from Californian and Australian models during the 1960s.

Inspired by the music of the Beach Boys and a run of Hollywood beach movies, surfing promised a hip and free seaside experience to teenagers who

spent hours in the waves mastering their technique.

That technique originated in Hawaii where the first Britons to see it were Captain James Cook and his crew of sailors. In a journal entry for 1779 Cook recorded how 'Twenty or thirty natives, taking each a long narrow board, rounded at the ends, set together from the shore. Their object is to place themselves on the summit of the largest surge, by which they are driven along with amazing rapidity [back] towards the shore...' The earliest record of anyone trying to surf in Britain dates from 1890.

Interest grew after 1914. A Jersey pioneer, Nigel Oxenden, travelled to South Africa, Australia and Hawaii after the First World War and having picked up surfing on the way he became a founder member of the Island Surf Club in 1923. Boards were mostly homemade and riders used their bellies more than their feet but by 1937 there was sufficient activity at Newquay for the Great Western Railway to use an image of a surfrider on their poster for the resort (see p. 146). Bude was another Cornish town that offered thin wooden boards for hire to holidaymakers who inevitably had their photographs taken attempting to use them. Locals made progress in the sport but the arrival of a team of Australian lifeguards at Newquay, with their performance fibreglass surfboards, in 1962 helped propel the town to its fabled status as Britain's 'Surf City.' It is now the centre of the UK's multi-million pound surf industry. ■

The earliest record of anyone trying to surf in Britain dates from 1890.

Lifeguards Flag

Bold red and yellow flags flapping in the salty air
denote safe bathing areas on a beach
that is patrolled by lifeguards.

They were first seen in August 1954 when twenty-two Cornish volunteers at Bude were awarded their Bronze Medallions by the Australian Surf Life Saving Association. They had been coached by Alan Kennedy, a stalwart of the Australian life saving scene who came to work in Britain in 1951. Having heard about the wonderful surf at Bude, from Australian airmen stationed at neary St Mawgen during the war, he was keen to share his experience for the benefit of local people. The necessary equipment of reel with modern nylon line, belt and surf ski, was sent from Australia and when the first batch of students took their examinations BBC film cameras were there to watch. Kennedy presented the red and yellow club colours that day when Bude Surf Life Saving Club officially came into being.

British efforts at beach life saving before this time had been mixed. From the 1860s drowning rates had taken a disturbing upward turn as more non-swimmers took to the sea in bathing machines. Without any formal procedures in place Victorian bathing women played an important safety role. Mary Wheatland of Bognor Regis, pictured on p. 19, had saved thirty lives and been awarded two medals by the time she retired aged seventy-four.

The establishment of the Royal Life Saving Society around the turn of the century helped prioritise the supply of lifebelts and ropes to seaside resorts. Until the 1950s their qualification was the only one recognised for beach life saving, though it had the serious drawback of being tested in still water. Rescuing people from the ferocious surf of stormy beaches required special skills so, following the creation of surf life saving clubs at St Agnes and Brighton in 1955, a national Surf Life Saving Club of Great Britain was formed. Their volunteers now patrol beaches throughout South West England and Wales with 240 more beaches coming under the remit of the Royal National Lifeboat Institute (RNLI). All use the red and yellow flags pioneered at Bude. ■

Caravan

Affordable caravans had a dramatic effect on postwar holiday habits. People could take their home comforts with them and even the prospect of meals out of tins and the infamous toilet tent proved minor drawbacks compared to the appeal of the open road.

The idea of touring for pleasure originated with Dr William Gordon Stables who travelled the country in his own purpose-built caravan in 1885. His exploits inspired a breed of upper class 'gentleman gypsies' who founded the Caravan Club of Great Britain and Ireland in 1907. With the interwar motoring revolution the caravan habit began to spread to middle class car owners. By 1933 car registration had passed the one million mark, doubling by 1939. Nonetheless, caravanning was still in its infancy; the real boom happened from the 1950s.

Not only were there too many holidaymakers chasing too few seaside beds, people also had more disposable income and a willingness to cater for themselves. Post-war assembly line manufacture made use of government surplus but the caravan industry rapidly moved on to using new plastic materials for cheaper, more lightweight models. Whereas the double-decker caravan with upstairs bedrooms proved short-lived, Alperson's 'Sprite', a simple 11 feet box on wheels, inspired an army of fans. In 1966 British caravan production hit 65,000 a year.

Caravan sites sprang up outside all the traditional resorts but, crucially, they could also be found on undeveloped stretches of coastline. Pioneering mobile home maker Willerby of Hull produced its first 'living caravan' in 1951 and these static models became an increasing feature of sites in ensuing decades, available to rent or buy. Seen from the air, their visual impact on our coastline is highly evident with notable concentrations in the South West, North Wales and Lincolnshire. By the late 1980s 90% of visitor bedspaces along the coast between Skegness and Mablethorpe were provided by caravans and chalets. Yet, like the Edwardian and interwar railway carriage bungalows that preceded them, caravan sites have the virtue of being essentially

temporary. Indeed, it could be argued that mobile homes are ultimately less damaging to seaside communities than the influx of more affluent holiday home owners who have inadvertently priced locals out of some of the country's most picturesque seaside towns and villages. ◼

By the late 1980s 90% of visitor bedspaces along the coast between Skegness and Mablethorpe were provided by caravans and chalets.

John Hinde Postcard

The Beach, Crantock, Cornwall.   Photo: E. Ludwig, John Hinde

During the 1960s and 70s the most vibrant postcards
in the racks of souvenir shops were produced by
Irish company John Hinde Ltd.

A pioneer in colour photography, Hinde set up his eponymous business in 1957, taking many of the early pictures himself. He set high standards and if it took a week for the right sky to materialise, his photographers were expected to wait. To get their trademark splashes of bright colour, photographers often went on shoots with a spare red pullover or potted flowers ready to plant in the foreground. Additional colours were added to the transparencies in post-production. Such was the appeal

Porthminster Beach and the Island, St. Ives, Cornwall.

Colour Photo by John Hinde, F.R.P.S.

of the John Hinde postcard that the company worked in twenty countries and recorded annual sales of over 50 million cards.

The company's peak years coincided with the era of mass tourism and some of the most captivating views highlight the new popularity of Devon and Cornwall. In 1968 the seaside still accounted for 75% of main domestic holidays but thanks to rising car ownership traditional resorts were now competing with the picturesque coastal towns of the West Country. Their stunning beaches and old fishing ports had previously been too remote from urban centres; now the lack of development became a key part of their appeal. In the 1970s

leaving the newly-built M5 to sit in traffic jams on narrow country roads became a rite of passage for holidaymakers heading west. Proof of this can be found on the back of postcards where people wrote more about the motorway services and the length of their journey than they did about their actual holiday.

John Hinde postcards infused with light and saturated with colour made Cornish beaches look every bit as good as anything the Continent could offer. At a time when cheap package deals were beginning to allow ordinary people to fulfil the aspiration of holidaying abroad this romanticised vision helped secure the popularity of a different kind of seaside. ■

Penzance Beach and the Harbour, St. Ives, Cornwall.

Lizard, England's most southerly point, Cornwall.

John Hinde postcards infused with light and saturated with colour made Cornish beaches look every bit as good as anything the Continent could offer.

Harbour Beach, St. Ives, Cornwall.

Inner Harbour, Polperro, Cornwall.

Windbreak

Bright blocks of colour among the *melée* of human activity, windbreaks have become a standard feature of British beaches.

Easily rolled up for carrying onto the sand, they are a simple yet functional combination of poles and fabric that when stretched out and hammered into the ground provide much-needed relief from sea breezes.

In the summer of 1939 the 'Sunnybouy Windodger' was advertised as 'The first beach shelter to make sunbathing possible in Britain.' Made of waterproof waxed canvas this windbreak was said to be 'designed on aerodynamic principles so that even a gale cannot blow it over.' It also featured handy pockets for holding bathing suits, towels and magazines. Sadly, wartime beach closures rapidly made production of the Windodger

Windbreaks are used to make family encampments like that pictured far left at St Ives in Cornwall. At Broadstairs in Kent, left, they have been stretched out against the prevailing breeze.

unviable and photographic evidence suggests that windbreaks did not actually become common until the 1950s, when they were made of striped canvas rather than the plastic tarpaulin more common today.

In 1971 the Welsh photojournalist David Hurn captured a group of stoic holidaymakers on the otherwise empty beach at Aberavon, Port Talbot sitting in deckchairs encircled by eight consecutive windbreaks.

In his picture the families have created their own defensive enclosure, keeping the wind at bay but also marking out their territory. Windbreaks are good for that, designating little family encampments that are easy for children to spot when they come back from building sandcastles or paddling in the waves. They also provide privacy when getting changed and on a windy day keep the worst of the sand out of picnic food and ice creams. ▪

Flip-Flop

These loose-fitting sandals get their name from the sound
they make when the sole of the foot hits the floor.

So simple is their two piece design, of flat sole and Y-shaped toe strap, that it has been worn by humans for millennia. Evidence of Ancient Egyptian flip-flops can be found from 4000 BC and the oldest known pair to survive are on display at the British Museum, made of papyrus around 1500 BC. Other cultures used the materials they found around them to fashion similar sandals; in the Far East this was rice straw, Indians employed wood and the Kenyan Maasai used rawhide.

The modern synthetic incarnation developed from the Japanese *zori* after the Second World War. The country's rubber industry played a big part in post-war reconstruction efforts and as designers experimented with updating the traditional Japanese sandal they found a ready export market in America where the flip-flop became associated with the casual Californian beach lifestyle of the 1960s.

Britons began wearing rubber and plastic flip-flops in the late 1950s and within two decades they had become standard holiday footwear, available from seaside shops alongside buckets and spades. The idea of specific beach shoes was not new, however. Victorian women wore straw-soled pumps that laced up the ankle which were superseded in the 1920s by slip-on rubber bathing shoes known as Dabs, available in a wide range of colours. The modern ubiquity of flip-flops is down to the fact that they are easy to get on and off, as well as being sand and water-proof. Their lightweight foam soles are cheap to mass produce making them highly disposable items. Unfortunately, beach clean-ups demonstrate that many have found their way into the oceans as plastic pollution. ◾

The modern ubiquity of flip-flops is down to the fact that they are easy to get on and off, as well as being sand and water-proof.

Clevedon Pier

John Betjemen described Clevedon as 'the most beautiful pier in England'. Its unique Grade I listing puts it in the nation's top 2.5% of historic structures. Nonetheless, in 1979, its Council owners voted for its demolition.

The fight to save Clevedon highlighted the plight of piers everywhere.

Stretching 842 feet (257m) from the north Somerset coast into the Bristol Channel, Clevedon Pier was built to withstand the second highest tidal range in the world. With an openwork wrought iron structure of eight graceful arches and a landing stage at the end, it opened on Easter Monday 1869. Unfortunately the resort around it failed to take off and by 1891 Clevedon Pier was in financial difficulty. Sir Arthur Elton bought it and donated it to the local council. In 1969 the pier celebrated its centenary with a pageant of people dressed in Victorian costume. Then disaster struck.

During a routine load bearing test in 1970 part of the pier fell into the sea. It soon became clear that the local community would have to impel its restoration and two years later the Clevedon Pier Preservation Trust was established. Around the same Brighton West Pier was also under threat; its private owners could not afford to maintain it, campaigners called for its restoration, the council refused to allow demolition but no public money was made available to keep it open. After decades of uncertainty fire and storm damage meant it could not be salvaged and

now only the merest skeleton of the pier head survives in the sea.

Clevedon Pier was luckier. In 1984 the award of a heritage grant set an important precedent for seaside piers being as worthy of support as historic churches and country houses. Eleven years later additional funding was provided by the newly established Heritage Lottery Fund and the fully restored pier was finally re-opened by Sir Arthur Elton's great-great-grandson in 1998.

As a result of battles to save these piers and support others at risk the National Piers Society was formed in 1979. One of its most successful initiatives has been to promote a 'Pier of the Year'. Clevedon has now won this accolade twice. ■

Blue Flag

©Foundation for Environmental Edu

Since its UK launch in 1989, the number of beaches
awarded the prestigious Blue Flag has gone up
from twelve to 201.

This global gold standard was created in 1985 as a pilot scheme to reward French coastal municipalities for good sewage treatment and bathing water quality. Today the annual certification also covers beach information and cleaning as well as provision of lifeguards, public toilets, rubbish bins and drinking water.

Meeting these targets requires significant investment meaning that remote and unspoilt beaches are less likely to fly the flag than major resorts. It was the latter, however, that most needed the wake up call and the Blue Flag Awards helped spur many resorts into action on the important issue of safe bathing water.

Drains may not be the most glamorous subject but their smell ensured Victorian holidaymakers were all too conscious of them. Across the country, urban infrastructure had failed to keep pace with rapid population increase and seaside towns were especially unprepared for the exceptional strain summer visitors placed on existing fresh water supply and waste water disposal. The resulting outbreaks of cholera and typhoid made a mockery of resort marketing that emphasised the health benefits of a seaside holiday. Sewers typically emptied their contents straight into the sea and if the outfalls did not extend far enough bathers found themselves dipping in diluted effluent as it was washed back towards the beach.

Addressing this situation took a disgracefully long time. In 1970 sewage from about 6 million people was being discharged into the sea or estuaries and in 1994 more than 80% of larger coastal towns were still dumping some untreated sewage off the coast. A small group of Cornish surfers set out to highlight the scale of a problem they saw on a daily basis and in 1990 Surfers Against Sewage was born in Porthtowan

Awards helped spur many resorts into action on the important issue of safe bathing water.

Village Hall. Their success was helped by the privatisation of English water companies, as well as key pieces of European Union legislation, but the proliferation of Blue Flag Awards is testament to the much-needed clean up of our national waters. ■

Tate St Ives

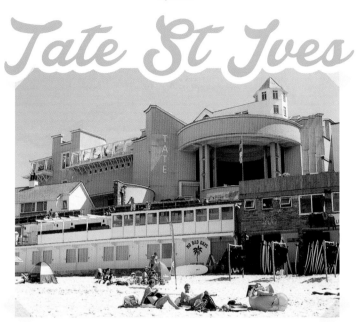

From the opening of Tate St Ives in June 1993 art galleries
and museums began to establish a stronger presence
at the seaside, attracting a different audience to coastal resorts.

Artists themselves had long valued the special qualities of light and the picturesque inhabitants of fishing communities, with the first painters drawn to West Cornwall after the railway extension to St Ives was completed in 1877.

With the establishment of an art school in 1880 painters came

from around the world, turning old working buildings into studios by the beach. James McNeill Whistler and Walter Sickert were early visitors but the appeal of St Ives was not restricted to painters. Bernard Leach and Shoji Hamada set up their pottery in 1920 and the presence, from 1939, of avant-garde sculptor Barbara Hepworth encouraged

a steady stream of modern artists to follow through the 1950s and 60s. In the late-1980s plans to create a gallery recognising these figures, as well as local self-taught maritime painter Alfred Wallis, began to take shape. Overlooking Porthmeor Beach the building designed by Eldred Evans and David Shalev featured a rotunda which echoed the shape of the old gas works it replaced. Visitor numbers in its opening year well exceeded targets and following a major extension that opened in 2017, Tate St Ives annually welcomes an average of 240,000 people.

Other artists colonies grew up at the Cornish fishing villages of Newlyn and Lamorna, as well as at Staithes in North Yorkshire.

These were categorically *not* seaside resorts, a fact which appealed to their artist residents. The reverse was true of Margate which already had a long seaside history when JMW Turner became a regular visitor in the 1820s, attracted by its glorious skies and seascapes, not to mention his relationship with seaside landlady Mrs Booth. Proposals to celebrate his links to the town came at a time when Margate's traditional visitor economy had dwindled dramatically. The opening of Turner Contemporary in 2011 therefore played a crucial role in regenerating the resort and its reputation. Modern art has also helped raise the profile of Hastings, following completion of the Jerwood Gallery, now Hastings Contemporary, in 2012. ■

Tate St Ives annually welcomes an average of 240,000 people.

Southwold Pier

Of the 100 or so piers built during the nineteenth
and early twentieth century, sixty one are still standing today.

Thanks to the Heritage Lottery Fund millions of pounds have been invested to safeguard the future of those at Penarth, Saltburn, Clevedon, Southport and Swanage. However, for the 56% of British piers in private ownership, the high maintenance costs must be met from profits.

Undaunted by this challenge, in 1987 Suffolk businessman Christopher Iredale purchased what was then the country's shortest pier at Southwold. Having grown up in London he became a self-confessed 'pier anorak' following a visit to Southend aged ten. With only loans to rely on, Iredale and his wife Helen overhauled Southwold's surviving pavilion with their own hard work and after five years set about realising their dream of reinstating the rest of the pier.

When it originally opened in 1900 Southwold Pier was 810 feet (247m) long. Steamers called on their progress around the east coast until the 1920s but Southwold was only ever a 'select' resort; for crowds and amusements holidaymakers went to Great Yarmouth or Clacton. After storms and ship collisions emasculated the pier in the 1950s locals simply accepted its loss. In 1999 work finally began on its reconstruction.

In the decades since new Southwold Pier was officially opened in July 2001, Mr Iredale's faith in the future of seaside piers has been more than repaid. Southwold was one of the earliest resorts to benefit from a resurgence of interest in the British coast, made trendy by its bright beach huts, unspoilt streets and good restaurants, not to mention the pervasive malty aroma supplied by Adnams Brewery. The pier capitalised on this reputation with quality eateries and quirky amusements custom-built by inventor Tim

Hunkin, including the water clock pictured below. By summer 2015 visitor numbers to Southwold Pier were approaching a million a year.

After storms and ship collisions emasculated the pier in the 1950s locals simply accepted its loss. In 1999 work finally began on its reconstruction.

Seafront Sculpture

By the late 1990s public art had begun to play a key part in seaside regeneration projects.

The preceding two decades had proved very difficult as access to foreign destinations made the traditional seaside holiday look deeply unfashionable. Promoting contemporary art and architecture emerged as a way to challenge that perception. By turning promenades into open air galleries, resorts of all sizes

transformed this key seaside location from a low brow into a high culture space available to everyone.

Trailblazing examples included the 1998 South Promenade Improvement Scheme at Bridlington which featured the *Nautical Mile*, a 1.9km pavement inset with text about the town's history. A year later the Queen unveiled Graham Ibbeson's statue of Eric Morecambe, part of a wider scheme for updating coastal defences along Morecambe Bay which also encompassed the TERN Project, a series of seafront sculptures celebrating local birdlife. Southport's promenade improvements included statues of Edwardian pier divers Professor Osbourne and Professor Gadsby that, like Blackpool's *Comedy Carpet*, celebrate the entertainment history of seaside resorts. The comic catchphrases written permanently into Blackpool's South Promenade are just one of many works commissioned there, another favourite being Michael Trainor's 6m diameter mirror ball that, as seen opposite, reflects aspects of the seafront in a completely unique way. In her mosaic of 'Esturiana', pictured right, Anne Schwegmann-Fielding used sea glass, beach finds and souvenir porcelain donated by residents of Harwich and Dovercourt, to create the Goddess of Creativity, Harwich and the Estuaries.

Elsewhere, big name artists have had a major effect on visitor numbers. Crosby beach, near Liverpool has become a tourist destination since the 100 standing figures of Anthony Gormley's *Another Place* were installed there in 2005. Damien Hirst's presence in Ilfracombe, with an art café and 20m high sculpture of *Verity*, pictured overleaf, whose skull and foetus are exposed above the harbour, has been similarly transformative. As local Shane Gooch told *The Guardian* in 2018: 'Art is subjective. You like it or you don't. But I do believe *Verity* and Hirst have changed expectations in the town. They've encouraged investment.

We've got smart restaurants and more galleries. Not so long ago the town used to feel a little downtrodden but there's a new optimism now.' The same can be said for the seaside more broadly. ■

Public art has helped the seaside feel like a vibrant place again. It has brought people back who would not have considered visiting the 'traditional' seaside. Long may it last.